眞劍道
Shinkendo

Japanese Swordsmanship

Photo by Pierre Yves Benoliel

Toshishiro Obata

International Shinkendo Federation
P.O. Box 2134,
San Gabriel, California, 91778

Published, designed and laid out by the International Shinkendo Federation, P.O. Box 2134,
San Gabriel, California, 91778
http://www.shinkendo.com
email to: shinkendo@aol.com
Printed in the United States
First edition, 1999

Cover/back photo: Itsukushima Jinja rendering courtesy of : Paul Couch
Shinkendo Japanese calligraphy on cover by Ueda Akio
Shinkendo kuyo no kurai rendering courtesy of: Kudo Muramasa, pg. 32
Shidachi for Tachiuchi : Obata Yukishiro
Technical photographs: Frank Klaver
Editors: Obata Yukishiro, Michael Esmailzadeh, & Dr. Deborah Klens-Bigman
Layout: Jorin Bukosky & Sammy Briggs

Obata, Toshishiro
        Shinkendo: Japanese Swordsmanship

ISBN 0-9668677-0-X (pbk.)

        1. Martial arts - Sports   2. Martial arts - Japan   3. Martial arts - History   I. Title

Other books written by this author include:
"Heiho Okugisho" (translation)
"Kama: Weapon art of Okinawa"
"Naked Blade: A manual of Samurai Swordsmanship"
"Crimson Steel: Samurai Sword Technique"
"Samurai Aikijutsu"

DISCLAIMER:
The publisher and/ or the International Shinkendo Federation (ISF), its members, Instructors or
affiliated branches WILL NOT BE HELD RESPONSIBLE for damages or injuries of any type as
a direct or indirect result of reading, practicing techniques or ideas presented in this book. This
book is designed to be an introduction into the sword art of Shinkendo, and as such is intended to
be used in conjunction with personal instruction under an ISF authorized Instructor. Instructor's
credentials, current status and ranks can be verified by contacting the ISF home dojo. Please use
common sense AND consult a doctor before undertaking any martial art or sport.

Shinkendo

Table Of Contents

Obata Jinja in Obata Machi. Established in the 3rd Century, now Gunma-ken Kanra-gun Kanra-cho Obata (Obata machi).

Special thanks are due to my dedicated students for their help in the production of this work, and to the family and friends who offered their patience and support.

Preface

This long awaited publication marks the first printed effort to disseminate the teachings and philosophy of Shinkendo to students all over the world. It has been several years in the planning, and I believe will prove to be beneficial to those who study it. While current students of Shinkendo will stand to gain the most from this book, practitioners of other arts will also find some principles in common, and possibly new principles previously unrealized.

All major aspects of Shinkendo are introduced in this first volume. However, because of space limitations, each of these aspects will need to be isolated and thoroughly explained in other books to follow.

Please keep in mind that studying from books and videos is not adequate, and qualified instruction should be sought by those seriously interested in pursuing swordsmanship or other martial arts. There have been many cases of injuries and accidents in swordsmanship in recent years, and it would greatly pain me for Shinkendo to fall victim to this unfortunate circumstance.

Jinsei Shinkendo / Life is Shinkendo!

Toshishiro Obata

Obata Toshishiro, 21 years old at the Meiji Shrine.

Author's Biography:

Obata Toshishiro, Shinkendo Founder

Obata Toshishiro was born in Gunma prefecture, Japan in 1948 of *samurai* family lineage. Raised in the countryside, he gained an understanding of body mechanics at a young age through outdoor activities such as chopping fire wood, climbing trees and running through nearby mountains.

At the age of 18, young Obata left his home and moved to Tokyo where he began his quest for expertise in the Japanese martial arts. It was at this time, that he applied for and was accepted as an uchi-deshi at the Aikido Yoshinkan under its founder Master Shioda Gozo and stayed for seven years.

Mr. Obata was fortunate to have trained in several renowned martial styles and traditions before leaving Japan; some of them being:

• Yoshinkan Aikido under Master Shioda Gozo
• Yagyu Shinkage-ryu under 20th generation Master Yagyu Nobuharu
• Ioriken *Battojutsu* under Master Uchida Tesshinsai
• Toyama-ryu and Nakamura-ryu Battojutsu under Master Nakamura Taizaburo
• Kashima Shin-ryu under Master Tanaka Shigeho
• Ryukyu *Kobudo* under Master Inoue Motokatsu
• *Juttejutsu* and Masaki-ryu *Manrikigusari* under Master Nawa Yumio

Other credentials and experience include:

• Founder of the Aikido & *Aikibujutsu* Tanren Kenkyukai
• Chief Instructor of USA Toyama-ryu *Battodo* Federation *Honbu*
• Chief Instructor of USA Nakamura-ryu Battodo Federation Honbu
• Chief Instructor of USA Bugekikai Aikido
• USA Battodo Federation Honbu
• Soshihan, USA branch of Nippon Battodo So Renmei
• Record breaking cut while performing traditional *kabutowari*
• 4 time champion at the Ioriken Battojutsu cutting competition
• 2 time champion at the all Japan Battodo cutting competition
• *Shitoka* (sword tester) for late swordsmith Kobayashi Yasuhiro
• Zen study under the Shiyukai group
• *Tateshi* (film choreographer) under Master Hayashi Kunishiro
• Curator for Japanese section of the W.M. Hawley private library

The Yoshinkan and Tokyo Wakakoma

As an *uchi deshi* at the Aikido Yoshinkan, Mr. Obata had the opportunity to instruct members of the Japanese Metropolitan Police; *kidotai* (riot police) as well students of the Nippon University and Obirin University.

Looking to expand on the sword work he had already been exposed to, Obata Soke cross-trained in several other arts, including the Yagyu Shinkage ryu style of swordsmanship. However, as an uchi deshi he was not able to pursue other arts seriously, and as a result concluded his 7 year apprenticeship at the Yoshinkan in 1973.

Mr. Obata was welcomed by the Tate Dojo to be a *bujutsu shihan*, and as such became a member of the Tokyo Wakakoma (an elite group of stuntmen, who also serve as fight scene choreographers for Japanese television and films), for which he was an instructorfor several years. It was necessary for members to research and learn techniques from different *bujutsu* in order to ensure the authenticity of action scenes and to diversify their stuntwork. These techniques included methods of archery from horseback, *sojutsu* (spear), various sword styles and the wearing of traditional clothing and *yoroi* (armor). Mr. Obata had the opportunity to train with many high level *budo* instructors during this time, and the knowledge and experience of these masters has proven instrumental in the development of Shinkendo.

Record Setting Kabutowari Test

In February of 1994 Obata Soke conducted a rare *kabutowari* (traditional helmet cutting test) using a sword forged in the Japanese fashion and a Hineno style black lacquer helmet (dated 1573-1602). The record length cut of 13 centimeters (4 sun, 3 bu) is currently the world record for testcutting an authentic Hineno style helmet (actual footage included in the "Shinkendo" video).

Establishing the Philosophy and Technique of Shinkendo

In addition to Obata Soke's own innovations, Shinkendo can be considered a unique, comprehensive re-unification of techniques and principles borrowed from other well-respected arts. The strongest principles of several martial styles have been incorporated into the curriculum:

Kendo - swift movement and reactions
Yagyu Shinkage-ryu and Kashima Shin-ryu - intensive sparring (*tachiuchi*)
Jigen-ryu - powerful strikes
Ioriken Battojutsu - swift and accurate *tameshigiri*
Aikido and Ryukyu Kobudo - fluid body movement

小幡利城真剣道開祖

Obata Toshishiro, Shinkendo Kaiso

1996

Shinkendo is a modern martial art, inspired by over 1200 years of samurai history, and *"bushi damashii"* (warrior spirit). From a physical standpoint, Shinkendo's techniques are taken from the practical methods once used by the samurai *(bushi)*. However, in addition to this catalog of techniques there are also a myriad of deeper teachings that can be discovered through a *shugyo* (serious, or austere) approach to practice. These include various ways of forging the mind and spirit in order to lead a more serious and rewarding life, development of a respect for nature and living things and the promotion of peace.

Practitioners are divided into *seito* (regular student level), *deshi* (certain serious, direct students), and *kyakubun* (senior ranked Instructors of other styles who would like to study). In Shinkendo, the *dan/ kyu* system of ranking is not used, rather, Shinkendo certification is based upon older ranking systems borrowed from the feudal era. Therefore, honorary *dan* ranks cannot be awarded.

Shinkendo's honbu is currently located in Los Angeles, California. While the accumulation of technique and rank takes time to develop and mature, Shinkendo has already experienced a pronounced increase of practitioners all over the world. Certain qualities are desirable in a student, and instructors should look for these when considering the student's advancement. The qualities include the spirit of *Jinsei Shinkendo* (life is Shinkendo - Shinkendo is life), self-reflection, and the goal to pursue self-development and purification of body, mind and spirit. Rather than criticizing others, students are encouraged to move in a forward direction through life, and be serious in all activities and endeavors.

Obata Soke teaches: *"Open up the friendship ring through the practice of Shinkendo, and through this training, learn to care for others and respect your elders. Patience and the feeling of continuity should also extend to everyday activities - not just saved for dojo practice".*

In Japan, to do something "Shinken" is understood as the intention to make a sincere, serious effort or attempt at an endeavor. This is the main reason the name Shinkendo was chosen.

Nathan Scott
Honbu Instructor

Part One

Japanese History and Martial Arts

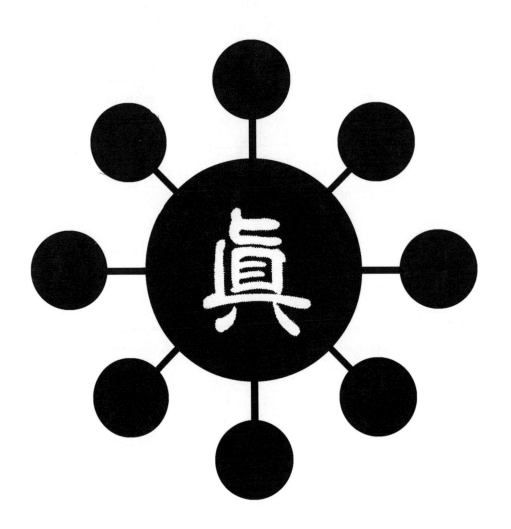

歴史の中の日本刀

Chapter One
The Sword In Japanese History

Obata family Akazonae (red armor)
displayed at the museum in Obata Machi.

The Sword In Japanese History

Yayoi era, Yamato era and Asuka era (3rd century - 7th century A.D.):
The history of the Japanese sword can be traced back to the beginning of the third century (end of the Yayoi era). In the year 239 AD, Queen Himiko controlled 34 territories called Yamataikoku. The beginning of the 4th century saw the ruin of Yamataikoku, and another power arose named Yamato Chotei. Recent excavations of ancient grave *kofun* (grave sites) from this period, show that the swords of this time were made of bronze.

In the year 607, the Crown Prince Shotokutaishi sent Ono-no-Imoko to China as an *kenzuishi* (ambassador). At this time, the blades made in Kure, an area located in southern China, were considered to be of the highest quality. Interestingly, the majority of ancient swords in Japan were originally either *kara-tachi* (Chinese swords) or *koma-tsurugi* (Korean swords). During this period, some *kara-kanuchi* (Chinese and Korean swordsmiths) moved to Japan, and the *yamato-kanuchi* (Japanese smiths) were strongly influenced by their methods and began forging their own swords in these styles. Blades of the Chinese style were called *Karayo-no-tachi* (Kara style), while blades of the Korean style were referred to as *Komayo-no-tachi* (Koma style).

Before the year 650, most swords were of the *hira zukuri* style (usually straight and flat, without ridgeline). It was after 650 that blades began to be forged with a curve, but the reason and exact time this happened is not recorded.

The late swordsmith Kobayashi Yasuhiro stated that a sword will tend to develop a curve naturally as a result of the steels cooling at different rates during the hardening/ quenching process of the cutting edge (differential hardening). Curved blades may have been created accidentally this way, at which time it is likely that smiths discovered that a curved edge cuts more efficiently and effectively than a straight edge.

Nara era (710-793 A.D.):
Sword styles included: hira zukuri, *kiriha zukuri, kissakimoroha zukuri* and some *shinogi zukuri* (which are still produced to this day). From the Nara era to the Heian era, diplomatic communications between China and Japan were severed and wars spread throughout Japan.

Heian era (794-1185 A.D.):
The straight sword continued to lose popularity, and the demand for the shinogi zukuri *nihonto* (curved Japanese sword) became stronger. The high quality of swordsmithing in Japan began to attract the attention of China and other countries. In 1167, the leader of the Heike clan, Taira-no-Kiyomori, became *Dajo Daijin* (prime minister) and ruled Japan. Although this was the first time a samurai had come into power, the political structure did not change from that set by previous

nobles. In 1180, another large clan, Genji, revolted against the Heike clan. In 1181, Taira-no-Kiyomori died of illness and after five years of hard fighting, the Heike clan was finally defeated and ruined by the Genji clan in Dannoura on March 3rd, 1185. Emperor Antoku, at the age of eight, died along with the Taira family, and the Emperor's sword (one of the three great treasures of Japan, bestowed to the Emperor) was lost in the sea of Dannoura.

Kamakura era (1185-1337 A.D.):

In 1192 the leader of the Genji clan, Minamoto-no-Yoritomo, became the first *Shogun* of the Kamakura era, and formed his *bakufu* (government) in Kamakura. Yoritomo started a political system run by samurai for the samurai class, and gathered a large group of swordsmiths in Kamakura to support his military. Some of the more notable smiths (*Toko* [those without disciples] or *Tosho* [those with disciples]) included Masamune, Sadamune, Yukimitsu, Shintogo, Kunihiro, and Kunimitsu, all of whom produced excellent blades. However, because of civil wars and the Mongolian invasions, many of these fine blades were destroyed.

In 1274 and 1281 Mongols tried to invade Japan, and were repelled both times. It was because of these invasions that the design of Japanese blades evolved dramatically. *Hamaguri-ba* (clam shell shaped edge) and longer swords were made to compensate for the Mongol's thick leather armor. Battle fighting tactics also changed from the traditional one-on-one style of combat to coordinated group battles.

Muromachi era (1338-1573 A.D.):

During this period, there were many wars, and Japan's fighting methods had changed due to the experience gained during the Mongolian invasions. In addition to a strong focus on the use of cavalry (something the Mongols were famous for), close range infantry fighting also increased in popularity. The long *tachi* was gradually replaced by the *katana* because of its ability to be drawn more rapidly.

In 1441, sixth generation Shogun Ashikaga Yoshinori was assassinated by the Harima Shugo (governor of Harima area), Akamatsu Mitsushige. After this incident, the Shogunate lost power and civil wars broke out. The last 100 years of Muromachi era involved the largest number of wars in Japan's history. As a result, this period was named the Sengoku Jidai (civil war era). During this time, *gekokujo* (the attaining of power through revolt) occurred, and position as well as rank were gained by lower ranking officials when higher ranking officials were killed in battle.

In 1573 - thirty years after guns were introduced to Japan, the Takeda clan fought the allied forces of Oda Nobunaga and Tokugawa Ieyasu at the battle of Nagashino. Takeda's cavalry of 15,000 highly trained and motivated men were believed to be Japan's strongest. Tokugawa and Oda had a combined 35,000 troops, including 3,000 firelock guns. Takeda's army lost 12,000 men to firearms alone. As a result of this battle, military strategists projected that the use of firearms would be the most important tactical element in future military campaigns.

Azuchi Momoyama era (1574-1602 AD):

Oda Nobunaga was almost successful in controlling all of Japan, but was assassinated by one of his retainers, Akechi Mitsuhide, at Honnoji temple, Kyoto in 1582. Akechi Mitsuhide was defeated in battle by Toyotomi Hideyoshi (a general under Oda) and was in turn killed while trying to escape only eleven days after Nobunaga's death by a farmer wielding a bamboo spear who was aspiring to be recognized by Toyotomi. Two days after Akechi was killed, Nobunaga's castle, Azuchi-jo, was burnt down. Eventually, Toyotomi unified Japan until his death in 1598.

Two years later Tokugawa Ieyasu and Ishida Mitsunari - a representative of Toyotomi Hideyoshi's son Hideyori, fought in the battle of Sekigahara. Ieyasu had approximately 100,000 men and Mitsunari had approximately 80,000. The battle began at 8:00am and by the afternoon Ieyasu defeated Mitsunari. Tokugawa's faction seized 25 percent of the land and resources, and he then assumed control of Japan.

Edo era (1603-1867 A.D.):

In 1603 Tokugawa Ieyasu became Shogun and established the Tokugawa Shogunate. The Tokugawa government lasted though 15 generations, spanning a period of 265 years.

•**1615:** Hideyori was killed during the Osaka summer campaign, and as a result of Ieyasu setting fire to Osaka castle many fine swords were destroyed. Some of the blades were re-tempered by the swordsmith Yasutsugu, but the rest were lost forever. The surviving blades were kept by the Tokugawa family in Owari.

•**1637:** Period of the Shimabara-no-Ran (revolt). Christians and villagers in Shimabara-han rose up against their *Daimyo*, Matsukura Shigemasa. The revolt was unsuccessful and cost the lives of over 40,000 christians.

•**1641:** Japan began to isolate itself from the influence of other countries (sakoku). A ban was placed on importing and exporting goods to and from Japan.

•**1657:** In January a massive fire broke out in Edo city (later named the "Meireki fire"). Over 60 percent of Edo was consumed including Edo castle's *Honmaru* (main structure) and with it some thirty crates, each containing thirty swords. Of the thirty crates, twenty-five (1051 swords) had been destroyed -only five crates were salvageable. The third generation of Yasutsugu effectively re-tempered several famous swords. The Honmaru of Edo-jo was never rebuilt.

•**1816:** The Toshogu shrine in Nikko, where Ieyasu was buried, caught fire and burnt down. Again, many fine blades were damaged by fire. Fortunately, the symbolic sword of Toshogu shrine, Sukezane, remained unharmed.

•**1853:** Commodore Perry landed in Tokyo bay. Civil war broke out between supporters of the Emperor (Satsuma, Chosu & Tosa clans) and the Shogunate.

•**1867:** Tokugawa Yoshinobu, 15th generation Shogun, resigned control of the government. As a result, the Tokugawa government was ruined, ending the long Shogunate rule.

Meiji era (1868-1911)

•**1868:** A new government was formed with the Emperor Meiji in power.

•**1871:** All samurai were required to cut off their topknots and conform to the standards of modern society. The wearing of swords was discouraged.

•**1876:** A new, stricter law was passed that ordered a ban on wearing swords in public. The sword was no longer considered symbolic of the samurai class.

•**1877:** The last civil war in Japan broke out, called "Seinan no Eki" (Seinan incident). Saigo Takamori, a samurai of the Satsuma clan, lead 30,000 men against the new government in an unsuccessful campaign. Saigo, after being shot in the thigh and stomach, committed *jiha* (ritual suicide). Swordsman Beppu Shinsuke performed *kaishaku* (beheading) .

•**1868 to 1945:** Three generations of Emperors ruled Japan during this period. In 1941-1945 during the second World War, major cities were burnt down by U.S. air raids, and important swords were lost or destroyed. As recently as the second World War officers still carried swords in keeping with the samurai spirit. Until being defeated in the second World War Japan's militaristic ideology had lasted 77 years - spanning from 1868 to 1945. After this time the Emperor declared that he was not in fact descendant of a god, but rather born of human lineage. Japan became a democratic country and began to look to America for matters regarding political policy.

The Japanese Sword

To the Japanese it is not an exaggeration to say that 'Japan is a land forged by the sword.' From mythological times the sword was considered one of the Emperor's three treasures. Swords can still be found in many king's graves as a symbol of power.

The sword was the samurai's main weapon, and it was also considered to be his soul. It was forged so that a samurai could defend himself, his family and his country with it. Samurai who distinguished themselves in battle often received a sword, and this usually became a family treasure to be passed down through the generations, reflecting the family's honor and history.

The steel used in making a Japanese sword contains many elements yet rusts very easily. In Europe coal was used to smelt sword steel, but the temperature used in this process was so high that unwanted impurities found their way into the metal. In Japan there was no coal, so charcoal was used (heated at a little more than 800 degrees). As a result of this, Japanese swordsmiths were able to put great effort into sword forging. Because the low temperature didn't cause impurities to melt as much, smiths were able to reduce the carbon content of their blades.

Japanese swords that are 800 to 1000 years old can be still be viewed in museums around the world. These swords usually have a history of being passed down through generations by many people, including high ranking generals and honorable warriors. Even though thousands of good swords were destroyed by wars, fire and various natural disasters; due to the efforts of conscientious people, there are still numerous fine blades remaining to this day.

There are certain characteristics of a nihonto (japanese sword) that are considered to be desirable. It is said that a sword should:

- •Be sharp   •Resist bending   •Not break (absorb shock)
- •Be appealing to the eye   •Be relatively light and easy to wield

Through the generations it has been every samurai's dream to have a good sword. Good Koto era swords have gone though many owners and many battles and many still remain to this day. However, blades of poor quality have not endured over the generations. It is believed that Koto blades have survived because they have been used in battle and proven to be of good quality. These swords, except those made thin from numerous polishings, have significant historical value.

It should be mentioned that every generation has had its share of high and low quality swords being crafted. *Shinto*, *shinshinto* and *gendaito* swords were made during peaceful times so some of them were crafted primarily as objects of beauty. While beautiful, these swords were often lacking sharpness and strength. There were still exceptional swordsmiths to be found during these periods, such as Kotetsu (Shinto period) and Kiyomaru (Shinshinto period).

Classification of Japanese Swords

Jyo Koto-before Heian period
Shinto- 1596-1763
Gendaito- 1868 - present

Koto-Late Heian period to 1595
Shin Shinto- 1764-1867

1. Tsurugi: Double edge straight sword - one of the Emperor's three treasures is a *tsurugi*. The tsurugi represents power. In the past it was thought that, while a person with power can control other people, this person will also be affected by and be responsible for the consequences of the use of that power. The double-edged sword philosophically represents *in-yo,* or *yin-yang* (equal positive and negative qualities). The blade edge faces you as well as the opponent, meaning that with the edge facing out people with power can control others through strength. But the opposite edge faces inward at the same time, implying that if you do not rule wisely the edge may pass judgement on you later. Many shrines have used the sword as their symbol throughout Japanese history.

2. Tachi: Over 2 *shaku* (60.6 cm) in length, single edged and curved. The tachi was the main weapon until the Sengoku era, and was slung on the left hip with the blade edge facing down to facilitate horseback riding. The tachi was worn during traditional Imperial and Shogunal ceremonies.

3. Katana: Usually more than 2 shaku (60.6 cm) in length. In use since the Kamakura era, but didn't become popular until the Sengoku era. The katana was worn blade edge facing up, thrust into the belt. The katana could be easily and quickly drawn and as a result became the main weapon for close-quarter combat. Samurai demanded swords to be sharp, as a dull sword would tend to break during battle, which could quickly alter the balance between life and death.

4. Wakizashi: 1-2 shaku (30-60 cm), held with one hand. Samurai always wore a *wakizashi* or *shoto* (short sword) to be used as a backup on the battlefield or for self-defense in the house or castle.

5. Tanto: 1 shaku (30 cm) or shorter, used for self-defense and when one needed to commit *seppuku* and jiha (suicide). *Tanto* were often given as wedding presents by Daimyo.

Gunto (Army and Navy swords)

The Imperial Army & Navy required its high ranking officers to wear gunto, and possession was closely managed by the government. Gunto are swords made specifically for the army and navy, the length of which were usually about 68cm. They could be used with either one or two hands.

These military swords had to be provided in such large quantities, that the quality suffered. Swords that have stamps, serial numbers, stainless steel blades, fake temper lines, or are machine made were created during the second World War, and are not looked on as true Japanese swords. These swords should be examined carefully, as many of them are very hazardous to use.

There are some gunto which were forged using traditional methods by swordsmiths, and are often of a grade high enough to be considered authentic Japanese swords. Nobuhisa and Yoshichika are examples of smiths who created good cutting swords during this time, and Miyairi Shohei in particular became a National Living Treasure. (Featured in the video "Molten Fire").

Modern Swords

After the second World War, swordsmiths changed their focus and began creating swords that were works of art, rather than being fully practical. While beautiful, these swords often do not cut well, lack sufficient sharpness, and in some cases are too highly tempered (causing the edge to become brittle and dangerous to the user and spectators if used for cutting). After the second World War, Japanese law restricted swordsmiths to forging a maximum of two long swords or three wakizashi a month, causing gendaito to become expensive collector items. When forged at high temperatures iron melts easily and the sword surface becomes beautiful, but the edge becomes fragile and cracks easily. Koto (old swords) are considered *meito*, or celebrated swords and are expensive because of their historical value and proven ability in battle. Nowadays, some swordsmiths have pride in their skill and traditions, but many have strayed from their basic objective: to create a sword that is beautiful, strong and sharp but doesn't bend or break.

Scene from "Ghost Warrior"
1983

武術　武道

Chapter Two
Bujutsu and Budo

Joshu mountain range, Gunma Ken

Modern Budo

Japanese martial arts have undergone drastic changes since the Meiji era (1868-1911). Traditional styles of martial arts were strongly influenced by the progressive changes in society and its new restrictive laws. The Meiji Restoration was enacted to promote modernization, foreign trade, and the abolishment of the feudal class structure. The restoration revoked the privileges of wearing swords and topknots by the samurai class, and as a result the study of swordsmanship was no longer unique to the samurai. Because of this the Japanese sword ceased to be the symbol of the "samurai." Since swords could no longer be worn in public interest in swordsmanship began to decline in popularity. The dramatic changes of the Meiji period created a void in which very few people practiced any kind of martial art. After Japan surrendered in 1945, bringing the second World War to a close, U.S. Army General MacArthur placed a ban on the instruction and study of all forms of military and martial arts (*gunpo* & *bujutsu*). The popularity of martial arts in Japan underwent a revival several years later with the re-introduction of *judo* and *kendo* as competitive sports.

Bujutsu and Budo

Japanese martial arts are often categorized as either bujutsu or budo. Although bujutsu and budo are different names, they have similar meanings. Bujutsu can refer to an art focussing on fighting technique and strategy, while budo could be thought of as emphasizing the spiritual/philosophical side of training and incorporating it into other areas of life. However, creating this kind of black and white division is misleading, and should be avoided. The spirit and state of mind of a practitioner has been considered an important element of martial arts since the creation of "*bu*" (martial arts). Also the extensions "*do*" (path, way of) and "*jutsu*" (technique, science of) have been used interchangeably for a long time. Japan opened its doors to European influence during the Meiji era, and this outside contact partially influenced the disuse of "jutsu" in favor of "do". Therefore, it would be more accurate to use the term bujutsu for those arts that originated previous to the Meiji era, and budo for those arts created after the establishment of the Meiji era. Both these terms should be understood to have the same meaning in a broad context. Common examples of this evolution of martial arts can be seen in the changes of *jujutsu* to judo, *kyujutsu* to *kyudo* and *aikijutsu* to aikido. In both bujutsu and budo, emphasis on spirit and technique has been and must be combined equally to deeply advance in a given art.

Zen

In modern times, the words Zen and spirit are often referred to excessively in relation to budo, while in fact, these concepts have become foreign to most martial arts. Strong budo must include spiritual and philosophical study as well as formidable technique. Spirit and technique go hand in hand and must be studied together to achieve "wholeness." Additionally, practitioners of budo should aspire to improve the condition of our society and world. Put another way, training in budo should enhance one's spiritual growth and be used to influence society and nature on a local and global scale.

Zen, an offspring of Buddhism, was first practiced in the year 1191 when Eisai founded the Rinzai sect. Rinzai Zen is the "Question-Answer" method, where one sits and interacts with the monks to understand oneself and the principles that govern reality. Rinzaishu Zen gained popularity among officials in the Kamakura government and high ranking samurai, and as such was protected by the Kamakura's 2nd and 3rd generation of Shogun (Minamoto no Yoriie and Minamoto no Sanetomo, respectively). Dogen created the Soto sect of Zen in the year 1227. This type of Zen focuses on the practice of sitting silently and meditating, with the hope that, over time, the adherent will finally understand the nature of reality, thus obtaining enlightenment. Both styles of Zen became popular during the Kamakura government, and greatly assisted in the spiritual training of samurai and Zen was thus inextricably linked to both bujutsu and budo. Zen taught understanding, patience, and influenced manners and behavior.

Later, the Sotoshu Zen sect developed, which consisted of sitting and allowing the mind to empty, at which state enlightenment could occur. The Sotoshu sect first became popular in Northern Japan, but eventually spread across the whole country.

Bushido

The study of the mind was also important for issues of morality and social manners. The way of the warrior, often defined as "bushido" in modern times, was the result of this study and adhered to strictly by the samurai class. Bushido included aspects of Shinto, Buddhism, Zen, Kogaku, Confucianism, Shingaku, heiho (strategy) and reiho (manner), and regulated the samurai's everyday way of living. bushido also included a background in swordsmanship, fighting/ military history, etc. The discipline of bushido was an important aspect of life in times of war as well as in times of peace. Although the meaning of the term bushido has varied translations, the fundamental principles remain the same.

Due to their above-mentioned historical ties, elements of bujutsu, Zen and bushido make up the underlying principles of budo. If these basic principles of budo are neglected, and only matters such as individual achievement and strength are sought after, then true budo cannot be experienced. Additionally, budo can be used to better oneself and others, or it can be used for committing acts of violence and crimes. Just as a policeman uses a gun to protect the people, criminals also use guns to attack others and perform crimes. Understanding this potential danger is important when selecting students, lest budo become associated with negative acts.

Part Two

真剣道教義

The Essence of Shinkendo

Chapter Three
Origin and Principles of Shinkendo

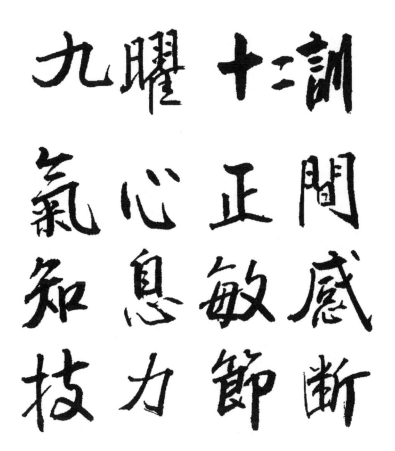

Shinkendo Kuyo Junikun

Ki	Shin	Sei	Kan
Chi	Soku	Bin	Kan
Gi	Riki	Setsu	Dan

Origin and Principles of Shinkendo

In feudal times swordsmanship was considered the core of the samurai martial arts just like the body's torso is the core of a person. Other military arts such as spear, archery, and unarmed combat were subsets of this core art, in the same way that legs, arms, and fingers are subsets of the body. With the exception of foot soldiers (usually recruited from villages and given minimal training) all persons of the samurai class were trained in swordsmanship, and would also specialize in archery or some other function.

The goal of Shinkendo is to develop the mind and body while learning an important cultural art, and then to apply these teachings and philosophies in everyday life. Serious training can enable one to discover the correct and proper path, using life skills found in the deeper levels of instruction.

The study of swordsmanship in modern times focuses not on simply "ways of killing", but rather serves as the founding principle and path to understanding Japan's samurai mindset, spirit and bushido. In the study of Shinkendo, the philosophy and strategy of the art is of paramount importance. An important principle is that of "Jinsei Shinkendo", or, Life is Shinkendo, mentioned previously.

Shinkendo philosophy consists of the principle "Jinsei Shinkendo" or Life is Shinkendo, the *Kuyo Junikun* and the *Hachido*. The twelve precepts of the Kuyo Junikun are *Ki, Shin, Sei, Kan, Chi, Soku, Bin, Kan, Gi, Riki, Setsu* and *Dan*. The Hachido (eight fold way) divides into:

1) *Ji* (oneself), *Ta* (others), *Shizen* (nature)
2) *Dai no Budo* (large martial art), *Sho no Budo* (small martial art)
3) *Jin Chu Ro* (center of the way, middle path)
4) *Zen, Aku* (Good and Bad)
5) *Kodo Keizoku* (action, continuation)
6) *Gojyo Goyoku* (five feelings, five desires)
7) *Jin Gi Chu Ko Rei Chi Shin* (the bushido code)
8) *Go Ju Ryu Ki Rei* (5 elements)

The Kuyo Junikun and sectionsof the Hachido will be discussed in detail later.

Shinkendo has a number of translations depending on the kanji (calligraphy) used to depict the various characters. Shinken is what a Japanese sword is called; however, shin can also mean true or serious, as in your pursuit of life and training. shin can mean mind and spirit, as the art affords you a way to forge both. Shin also means God, as understood to mean respect for our world and nature, and espousal of world peace.

Training is divided into basic, intermediate and advanced, and emphasize precise technique and safety as well as sword care and proper etiquette. An understanding of etiquette includes not only appropriate manners when conducting public demonstrations and training in the dojo, but also guides one's interactions with oneself, others and nature.

Shinkendo equally emphasizes these five important aspects of swordsmanship practice:

Gorin Goho Gogyo

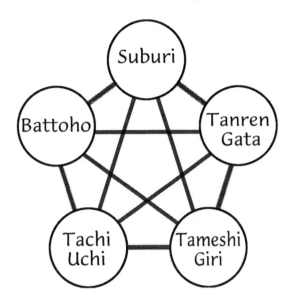

1. **Suburi** (swinging) practices *taisabaki* (body movement), *ashisabaki* (foot work), *kensabaki* (sword movement) and, *tohojussinho* (basic ten sword methods).
2. **Battoho** (drawing methods) are incorporated in the *Goho Battoho* tech niques, and emphasize drawing and sheathing in all directions.
3. **Tanrengata** (solo form) uses suburi in set forms to learn different types of footwork, body movement, turning movement, hip twisting, circular movements, and the focal point of the body.
4. **Tachiuchi** (sparring) adds an element of reality, and helps two individuals in obtaining a sense of harmony and timing by adjusting the distance, *kiai*, rhythm, strength and speed of techniques.
5. **Tameshigiri** (testcutting) uses toho jusshinho (explained in the tameshigiri chapter) to offer practical insight into principles such as *hasuji* (edge-angle), *tachisuji* (sword swing-angle), *tenouchi* (grip) and, against a non-moving target.

In addition to Obata Soke's own stylistic innovations, Shinkendo also utilizes certain techniques and elements borrowed from classical Japanese martial traditions. It is interesting to note, however, that there are certain advantages a modern martial art has over most extant classical traditions. Generally, A modern art is more at liberty to research and develop techniques and principles, whereas practitioners of *koryu* bujutsu, or classical martial traditions, often feel obligated to learn and pass on teachings exactly as they were instructed - even at the risk of passing on mis-interpretations. This is a perspective that has been largely overlooked by Budoka in the past.

"Senki"
Writen by Miyamoto Musashi (1584-1645)

真剣道九曜十二訓
Chapter Four
Kuyo Junikun

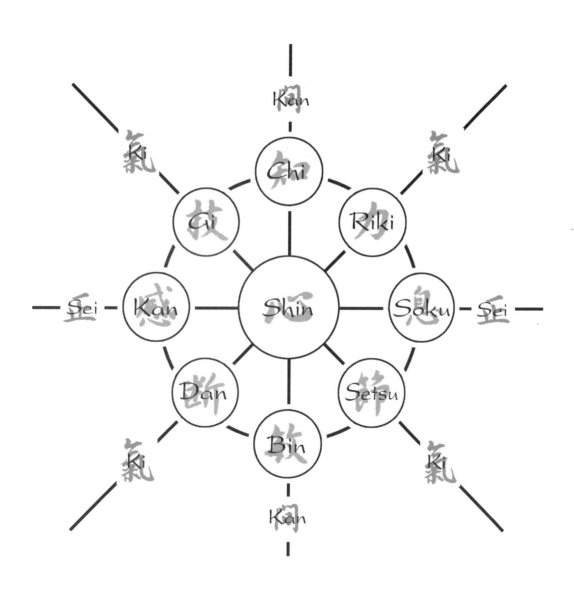

真剣道九曜の位

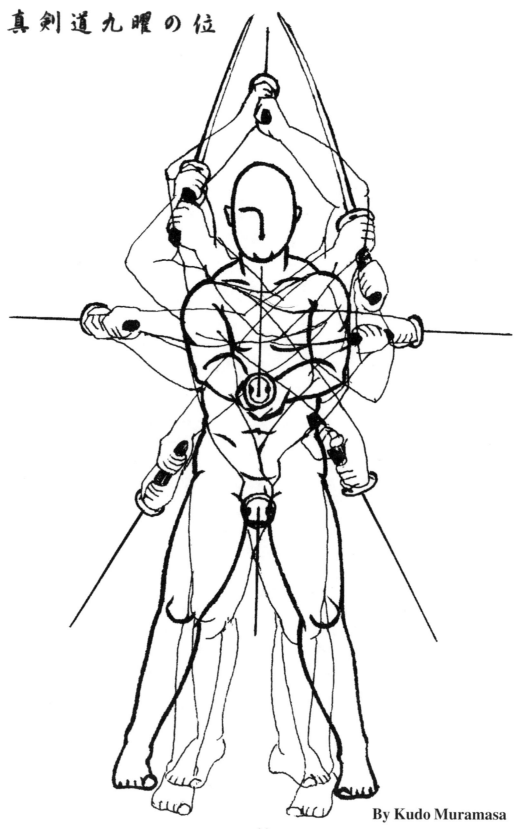

By Kudo Muramasa

32

Founding Principles Related to Kuyo Junikun:

身 心 の 鍛 錬

Shin-Shin no Tanren: *Training the body, mind and spirit*

The martial arts are unique, in that training emphasizes both physical and intellectual development. It is important to keep in mind that a human being is composed of body, mind and spirit, and as such all three must be continuously stimulated to maintain long term good health.

The human body can be divided into 3 major classes:

1) Flesh and bone   2) Organs   3) Brain

All three classes are related and interdependent, and as such they must co-exist in a state of balance; both mentally and physically. During training, it is important to be aware of this in order to achieve maximum strength and efficiency. The flesh and bone can be easily conditioned by rigorous physical training. The organs, however, are more difficult to condition and maintain. Poor eating habits or breathing smoggy/ contaminated air contribute heavily to organ damage, so proper diet and an awareness of these types of hidden dangers is crucial. The brain controls the internal organs, as well as the flesh and bone. It must be conditioned in ways that will promote strong will power and mental stability. Through training and retrospection, one can develop the ability to clearly distinguish right from wrong, good from bad, and discern which path of life is correct for them.

大 の 武 道　　小 の 武 道

Dai-no-Budo, Sho-no-Budo: *Large martial way, small martial way*

Budo, or martial arts (way), can be divided into two broad categories of dai (large) and sho (small). These are two basic perspectives in which the science of Kuyo Junikun can be implemented. Dai-no-Budo literally refers to combat; specifically in terms of large battles and wars. In the event of a military conflict, the dai concept should be applied to ensure victory. Even in times of peace, the Dai-no-Budo perspective can be utilized to control and govern the country properly. Areas of focus would include politics, management of society, methods of embankment, engineering, and quality of life. Dai-no-Budo can also be thought of as the strategy of life, which focuses on methods of accurately and decisively planning for the future, thereby improving the quality of one's life.

Sho-no-Budo essentially refers to one-on-one, or individual combat. The same concept can be applied to daily life and the careful management of one's self. The objective of Sho-no-Budo is to win against one's self or an opponent through the incorporation of confidence, patience, discipline, honor and decisiveness. As the understanding of Sho-no-Budo increases, undesirable circumstances that may result in violent conflicts or other hazards may be avoided. A proponent of Sho-no-Budo will experience an increase in awareness, alertness and cautiousness.

If Sho-no-Budo is put in the context of living life day to day, then Dai-no-Budo corresponds to ways of planning for the future. Sho-no-Budo refers to one's self, or the present, while Dai-no-Budo refers to a larger group of people or a wider frame of time (past and future).

Shinkendo practitioners should delve deeply into the concepts of Sho-no-Budo and Dai-no-Budo and use them to incorporate Kuyo Junikun into their lives.

Kuyo Junikun: *twelve precepts of the nine planets stratagem*

Kuyo Junikun is the basic, proprietary philosophy of Shinkendo. The twelve points of study are:

Ki Shin Sei Kan	Chi Soku Bin Kan	Gi Riki Setsu Dan

These precepts represent the collective elements that, when balanced correctly, generate spiritual, intellectual and physical strength and stability (personal development). Collectively they are a formula that can be used to create new ideas, and guide the actions that people choose. In accordance with nature's laws, each of the twelve precepts also contains within them the balance of yin/yang (in/yo, in Japanese), or, good/bad, strong/weak, positive/negative, etc. Since one cannot exist without the presence of the other, effort should be made to distinguish the difference. Both yin and yang have advantageous and disadvantageous properties, and to understand and apply this, one will succeed in finding and staying on the correct path. Students that seriously dedicate themselves to Shinkendo and learn these twelve precepts will inevitably increase their overall development.

In our solar system, there are nine planets that orbit the sun. Each planet has a unique orbital path and velocity that provides it with a harmonious co-existence with the other planets. Not unlike our solar system, a human being can also be thought of as a center point in which the twelve precepts revolve around and exist together in harmony. To neglect or lose focus of any of these points will result in an unbalancing of the orbit. If the points become too unbalanced, the whole system will fail; causing serious repercussions. Unfortunately, people are influenced by the negative energy of others, so Shinkendo practice provides a method of remaining focused and true to one's self. Adherents should continuously evaluate and seek to improve themselves by using these guidelines.

The twelve precepts should also be applied to methods like Sho-no-Budo, Dai-no-Budo, and can be used for general decision making, everyday living and any other areas the student of Kuyo Junikun deems important.

Outline of Kuyo Junikun's twelve precepts:

 1. Ki-energy

People, animals and nature give off energy. It should be the goal of all people to put forth positive energy, which will in turn aid in receiving positive energy from others. Positive thought directly influences the amount of positive energy acquired, while negative thinking drains one of energy and is self defeating.

 2. Shin-mind, heart and spirit - determination, resolve

To diligently strive for a strong, firm mind and enhancement of spirit. Also describes the qualities of the personality, character and emotional composition; including morals, courage and compassion (heart). The study of shin produces a pure, unfettered mind, able to develop sound morals and ethics. One should forge strong will power (spirit) in order to overcome negative temptations and failure.

 3. Sei- accuracy and precision

Every task or endeavor should be done with accuracy and precision ("if it's worth doing, it's worth doing right"). Skillful observation and evaluation of available information is of paramount importance in all dealings.

 4. Kan-   a) distance in space   b) distance in time

Keeping proper, advantageous distance. The ability to accurately judge distance in space (between physical objects) or time is important in any circumstance or endeavor. Distance in space also refers to perceived distance, as felt between two people; close or distant, smothered or comfortable. Distance in time (timing) should be considered when making decisions regarding business, social issues, or any other venture.

 5. Chi- intelligence, knowledge and wisdom

Look, listen, experience and understand (external cognizance). Wisdom is born from a combination of gained experience and the comprehension of information.

 6. Soku-breathing and respiration - breath control, rhythm

Oxygen and breathing are understandably an important part of a healthy life, and proper respiration is closely related to ki and general health. Soku also relates to rhythm and timing, used subconsciously in daily activities.

7. Bin-speed, agility, quick reaction.

The practice of performing tasks promptly and efficiently. To seize the moment. In a smaller context, to react quickly to another person's movements, ideas and thoughts; sharp reflexes.

 8. Kan-5 senses - perception

Training the five senses is crucial to all areas of life. It is possible to improve the performance of these senses through proper training, at which time "*rokkan*", the sixth sense of intuition and premonition can be cultivated. Kan provides deep insights to events or actions, and allows one to see past physical appearance and perceive the non-tangible. Use kan (internal cognizance) to improve learning skills and foster a deeper understanding of experiences.

 9. Gi-technique, methodology, skill

All knowledge is gained from experience or observation of one's self, others, and nature (ji, ta, shizen). After the process of researching, comprehending, and reaching a conclusion, use gi as a means of achieving one's goal.

 10. Riki-physical and mental power

Humans possess intellectual strength as well as physical strength. One type of riki can be used to influence professional and social activities, while another may be used to overcome obstacles or improve concentration. A person must always continue diligently to achieve the highest level of physical strength and mental faculties.

 11. Setsu-accumulated experience, sequential process

Time is an accumulation of years, months, days, hours, minute and seconds. Each second adds to the rhythm of time, which leads to the passing of seasons. Thus, it is natural that one should also build a foundation using a step by step process of stacking experiences, rather than by jumping ahead. While it is important to consider the past and future, the focus on the present time should take precedence.

 12. Dan-decisiveness, judgement

Decisions, both small and large, are a constant factor in life. Use good judgment to establish the necessary parameters in which clear, accurate decisions can be made. Decisions and the ability to judge objectively are fundamental skills.

自 力　　他 力　　自 然 力
Jiriki　　Tariki　　Shizen ryoku
Ji, Ta, Shizen - One, Others and Nature

It should be the ambition of all people to live in and contribute to society, harmoniously interacting with others and remaining aware of nature. Nature is responsible for air, water, food, shelter and all the elements needed for basic human survival. All things of this earth exist and thrive in accordance to the natural laws of physics, and as such it is damaging to neglect or live outside of these laws. History has shown us that to destroy or attempt to modify these principles of nature will prove disastrous.

The media and society attempt to influence behavior and actions through overt and subliminal suggestion, so one must have the ability to decide what is right for one's self. The study of ji, ta, shizen provides a method of keeping perspective, and a reference for applying/ contemplating actions and strategies.

自 力　1. *Jiriki*-self powered (one) intent; the ability to observe, feel, formulate, and understand. Conclusions and decisions are based on this information.

他 力　2. *Tariki*-outside (others) influence; from other people. What other people say and do influence one's own actions and beliefs (in positive and negative ways).

自 然 力　3. *Shizen ryoku* -(nature) natural elements, such as time, season, environment, temperature, weather, implements, clothing etc.

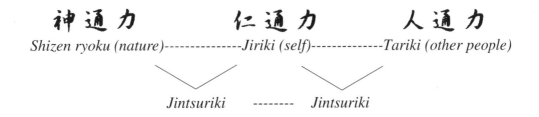

神 通 力　　仁 通 力　　人 通 力

Shizen ryoku (nature)--------------*Jiriki (self)*--------------*Tariki (other people)*

Jintsuriki　--------　*Jintsuriki*

Jintsuriki = Above average capacity and ability. Combining these principles will provide better insight to the workings of people and the world. Jintsuriki can be used to create a "Supernatural Power" and influence others in positive ways.

礼法

Chapter Five
Etiquette

Obata Kaiso in Australia, 48 years old.

Dento

According to Japanese thought, *dento* (tradition) is composed of *seido* (system, method), *fuzoku* (manners, customs) and *shiso* (thoughts, ideas). In both the English and Japanese language, tradition is the handing down of customs, methods of practice, and systems of thought through the generations. For hundreds of years in Japan, *budoka* have passed down martial art principles and techniques to students in this way, thus providing a future for their art. However, as a tradition is passed down the techniques require some degree of adaptation to prevent the style from stagnating. To neglect these aspects condemns an art to an existence as a historically significant cultural asset, as opposed to a living, growing tradition. Yet in order to alter techniques or patterns while staying true to the underlying principles of an art requires that the new generation deeply understands the founder's theory, application and physical technique. For example, in swordsmanship there is a standard grip taught by most schools. This grip is effective in most cases, but less so in special cases, such as when the tang is significantly shorter than the end of the hilt. Too wide a grip can cause the wooden hilt to break under the stress of cutting. Consequently, an informed swordsman should take the construction and specifications of a given sword *as well as* their own physical composition into consideration when practicing. This adaptation is representative of an understanding of core principles, or theory, and should serve as the basis for innovations by modern budoka.

Historically there was a constant need for stylistic modifications. During the Genpei era the warrior's kabuto (helmet) was very wide and richly decorated. However, with different methods of warfare becoming common toward the end of the Muromachi era, the need for a more practical kabuto became necessary. The result was a smaller, less decorated kabuto with it's primary purpose being that of combat efficiency. With the change of the kabuto's design, kamae (sword posture) and technique evolved with it. Techniques were also adapted to provide for the difference between those opponents wearing light armor and those wearing heavy armor. During the Edo era, a period of general peace, elements of swordsmanship such as kamae, blocking and attacking began to change due to the decrease in the use of armor.

In modern times, some budoka are quick to criticize each other's styles. Such critiques are meaningless unless one has researched the history of the style to understand what course of events led to a given style's curriculum. Before the Sengoku era, when tachi style swords were in use, one could sit on a *shogi* (stool) or directly on the floor without fear of damaging the *saya* because the tachi was carried edge-down, hung 15 cm below the waist belt by a cord. The tachi was carried in this fashion with or without armor and was easily drawn from an upright or sitting position. As time passed, fighting styles underwent dramatic changes. Swordsmanship evolved from use of the tachi to the katana, the latter of which was developed and favored for its advantageous edge-up carrying position in the waist belt allowing it to be drawn quickly. During this time, schools of etiquette required samurai to wear *daisho* (long sword and short sword) while in public. Indoors, samurai wore the wakizashi (short sword; also called "companion sword") at all times, while storing the katana (long sword) on a *katanakake* (sword stand). When visiting another person's home the formal sitting position was *seiza* (kneeling) with the katana by one's side on the floor. To wear the katana while in seiza was considered inappropriate, cumbersome, and invariably caused the tip of the saya to rub on the floor. Placing the katana by one's side on the floor comfortably within reach solved that problem, while still allowing the owner to draw it quickly if necessary. Historically the only long sword worn indoors was the tachi, which one used a type of cross-legged sitting position with.

Interestingly, Japan's armed forces decided to change from the Japanese style sword to the European style sabre in the period of time between the Meiji and Taisho era. During a cavalry battle with the Chinese army, the Japanese army cut down 370 horsemen with these sabres. However, on returning the next morning, it was discovered that only 50 out of the 370 horsemen cut had actually suffered fatal wounds. The sabre was not sharp enough to cut efficiently, and due to its one handed design, could not be used as strongly or effectively as the katana. A certain Lieutenant Kurihara was reported to have infiltrated an enemy bunker with his Japanese sword and killed 18 enemy soldiers. Soon after this incident, the Japanese sword design was again recognized by the Japanese military as the world's most effective two-handed sword.

Etiquette

During the Kamakura era to Muromachi era, many schools of etiquette were developed. Among them were the Ogasawara-ryu, Ise-ryu, and Ujitaka-ryu. During the Edo era the Tokugawa government designated Ogasawara-ryu as the official style of etiquette. This was because Ogasawara Sadamune (1291-1347), the founder of Ogasawara-ryu, was a samurai and had formed his style around the needs of samurai. Methods of greeting, walking, turning corners, opening doors, entering buildings, drinking and eating were all modified in consideration of the Japanese sword. Etiquette was further dictated by strategic considerations such as sword distance, position, and time needed to ensure one's own safety and that of others. These methods later evolved to focus primarily on the qualities of dignity, respect, simplicity and beauty. Other classes of people such as farmers, craftsmen, and merchants, admired samurai manner and began to adopt these methods as well. Eventually, Ogasawara-ryu spread throughout Japan, resulting in it eventually becoming the style of etiquette used by all Japanese people.

Kiritsu - Standing with sword.

The proper standing position requires one's heels to be together, toes angled outward 35 degrees (creating an inverted triangle between the feet), back straight, chin tucked and the sword to be carried on the right side while using the thumb to hook the tsuba (sword guard) at all times for safety. The *sageo* (sword fastening cord) should be divided into three equal sections, and the last third of the sageo should be held between the index and middle finger of the right hand. This grip allows for one to retain the sword, through the use of the sageo, even if the sword is accidentally dropped or struck loose. The elbow should be lightly bent, thus raising the sword to waist height. This provides a range of movement (shock absorption) that can prevent the sword from being pulled or struck out of one's hand.

Torei - Bowing to sword (from standing)

When bowing to the sword, the right hand should support the *tsuka* (hilt), as in *kiritsu*, while the left hand supports the saya (scabbard) tip. The sword should be horizontal and at eye level. This method is a sign of respect and protects the sword from one's breath and involuntary sneezes. Bow from the waist about 15 degrees, while being careful not to adjust the position of the sword.

Zarei - bowing with sword from a kneeling position

To assume the proper position for bowing, one should kneel down on both knees; first left, then right. The knees should be comfortably apart to provide a stable foundation with the big toes either slightly touching or overlapping. The back should be kept straight, chin tucked, and both hands should be placed diagonally on the upper thighs, fingers together. The sword should be parallel to the direction the user is facing, and the tsuba in line with the front of the right knee.

Placing the sword on the right side of the body, at least one shaku (30 cm) away from the right leg and blade edge facing inward, is appropriate when persons of seniority or higher status/ importance are present. This creates a non-threatening, respectful atmosphere. From the right side, one would need to first move the sword to the left side and change hands before being able to draw it effectively.

When it is appropriate to place the sword on one's left side, such as during training (or by medieval messengers on missions), the same basic etiquette is applied. However, from this position the sword should be placed within one shaku of the left leg, blade edge facing outward. Having the sword available on the left side is advantageous should the need arise to use it quickly. The sword can easily be picked up with the left hand and drawn with the right hand from this position.

There are many variations of the seated bow that differ from school to school. The most common method is to first slide the left hand forward, then the right hand, making a triangle in the space between thumbs and index fingers, directly in front of oneself. Bow from the waist, keeping the head in line with the back, to a position slightly above the floor (approximately five inches). Then, raise slightly while still looking downward and return both hands to their original position on the upper thighs; first right hand, and then left. Traditionally, drawing the right hand back first demonstrates caution, as one can still perform a right handed cross draw with the tanto or wakizashi in case of an emergency.

In formal Japanese etiquette, it is considered rude to look up at another person while bowing. The purpose of bowing is to show respect in a dignified, respectful manner. If it is necessary bow to or face someone who is unknown or not trustworthy, then adequate distance should be established. This method is also appropriate during practice, when possible, and is demonstrative of *zanshin*.

Additionally, proper manners dictate that the person opposing you should not be able to see the back of your neck while bowing, therefore a bow is performed with the torso, as opposed to the head.

Tachirei - standing bow

1. *Bowing to the flag, Emperor, President, shrines or churches.* The sword should be carried on the right side, but gripped *opposite* to that of kiritsu. The right grip should be place in the area between the sageo and *koiguchi* (saya mouth) . The edge is faced down at a 45-degree angle, and the tip of the sword should be facing downward.

2. *Bowing to the instructor.* The sword should again be carried on the right side. The blade edge should be facing up, and the tsuka forward. (kiritsu)

3. *Bowing to students, partners, or someone of equal rank.* The sword should be carried on the left side. The blade edge should face up, and tsuka forward.

General considerations for bowing

The distance between two people bowing should be that of a standard *tatami* floor board length; 1.8 meters. This is the ideal distance to face someone, because should the other person decide to initiate an attack, he or she would need to take more than one step forward to be in striking range. This would give one time to prepare for the attack. Additionally, when bowing to someone of equal rank or position, both should raise their heads simultaneously. Those bowing to one senior to them should raise their heads slightly after that of their senior's, to show proper respect and recognition of position.

Part Three

真剣道　技の部

Shinkendo Techniques

Shoro - temple belltower

Chapter Six
Overview

OVERVIEW

Ashisabaki - footwork
There are three basic types of footwork:

     1. Shuffle: *Suri-ashi*
     2. Step: *Hiki-ashi, Fumikomi-ashi, Fumikae-ashi, Hiraki-ashi*
     3. Pivot: *Kaiten-ashi*

    All foot movements can be considered a combination of these three types of footwork. In everyday life, a step (walking) is the most common and basic of leg movements. However, in Shinkendo the shuffle-step is considered the most basic footwork. Shuffle-steps allow one to adjust *ma-ai* (combative distance) cautiously over short distances. Suri-ashi's principle is to provide stable, low balance through the adjustment of footwork, and can be applied to all stepping methods. For example, to move forward 1 1/2 ft with the front foot while advancing 1/2 ft with the back foot would be one application. Students should practice shuffling, stepping and suri-ashi methods using wide, large movements as well as short, shallow movements in all eight directions. Kaiten-ashi requires one to pivot on the leading leg (clockwise or counter-clockwise) while extending the trailing leg, and utilize power from twisting the hips. This method of pivoting is very beneficial. All the above movements should be practiced exactly, yet at the same time with balance and fluidity.

    Advanced footwork includes such variations as *nuki-ashi* (pulling-step) and *nusumi-ashi* ("stealing" step).

Isshin-Nishin
    There exists a concept called "*Isshin - Nishin*" (mind/spirit - body), which refers to the coordination of perception, evaluation and reaction. The first element is to feel (perceive) a given situation. Second, one should see (evaluate) the variables of the circumstance. Finally, an accurate, decisive movement (reaction) can be performed. Isshin-Nishin should be researched and applied to optimize the outcome of any situation.

Jin Chu Ro (human, center/middle, way)
    Jinchuro means attacking the opponent's center of movement with one's own center. The first step in applying jin chu ro is to practice swinging the sword directly down the center line of the body. Following this principle, *uchidachi* can then simply adjust their center of movement to line up with *shidachi*'s center, providing powerful and effective technique. Uchidachi's center will become shidachi's center. Training in straight cuts will also help develop strong tenouchi and *tome*.

Tenouchi - grip

To check proper gripping of the *bokuto*, assume the position of seiza, sitting on the heels with the toes standing. Lower the bokuto to gedan no kamae, sword tip resting on the floor. After checking to see that the wrists are properly rotated inwards (*shibori*), apply pressure to the tip of the sword to test the strength of the grip. Correct grip, with the *goukoku* (web between the thumb and first finger) of both hands centered over the back of the blade, will allow the pressure of the cut to conduct up the arms, whereas an incorrect grip will cause weakness across the thumbs.

Blocking

In tachiuchi, it is important to keep the elbows close to the body while blocking. Neglecting this rule will allow an opponent to cut the exposed elbows.

Unnecessary movement of the sword tip should be avoided to maximize efficiency of speed and timing.

Batto - drawing

1. Before drawing the sword, loosen it from the saya (*koiguchi o-kiru*) by applying pressure to the back of the tsuba with the left thumb. *Caution: do not position the thumb or any other finger over the edge of the blade when drawing!*
2. When drawing, care should be taken not to introduce any twisting of the blade. The back of the blade should glide smoothly along the inside of the saya. Blade angle changes will mar the inside of the saya, and can prevent a clean draw.
3. Pull the saya back slightly while drawing to facilitate clearing the koiguchi.
4. Beginners should draw carefully and watch the koiguchi.
5. Draw the sword *completely* out of its saya before swinging. This is very important, as failure to do so may result in splitting the saya and possible injury.
6. Draw completely before releasing the saya with the left hand.
7. After practice, remove the sword and gently tap the mouth of the upright saya against the floor to remove any loose wood chips. Inspect the inside for damage.
8. Saya will tend to wear thin near the edge-side of the koiguchi over time. This should be checked, and reinforced (internally and/or externally) if needed.
9. If ordering a new saya, have it modified so that the edge-side has thicker wood, or have the outside of the saya between the koiguchi and *sageo ana* reinforced with copper, leather or shark skin.
10. It is also strongly advised that an additional *mekugi* (retaining pin) be fitted on all *iaito* and katana used for practice or demonstration.

*After a student has sufficient practice with batto and *noto*, drawing and re-sheathing the blade without watching the sword should be encouraged.

Noto - resheath

1. New students should begin practicing with bokuto before advancing to an iaito.
2. Alternate bokuto and iaito practice to ensure clean technique.
3. Completely encompass the opening of the koiguchi with the left hand; left thumb and index finger overlapping. *Do not extend the fingers along the blade!*
4. Re-sheath the sword by touching only the last 1/2 or 1/3 of the blade to the left hand (covering koiguchi). Catch the tip in the koiguchi, line up the saya and blade so that they are matched.
5. Slide the back of the blade along the inside of the saya.
6. Noto slowly and precisely. Be careful not to let the sword guard slam against the saya while re-sheathing. Careless re-sheathing can cause injuries such as thrusts or cuts to the hand, arm and stomach.

Chiburi - "blood flicking"

A. Jodan Chiburi   **B. Chudan Chiburi**   **C. Gedan Chiburi**

Jodan chiburi, or upper-level chiburi, is initially executed in three counts. While executing this chiburi, care should be taken not to swing the sword too close to the head, as injury from the blade edge or Tsuba is possible. Chudan chiburi, or midde-level chiburi, is executed with the right foot forward. Gedan chiburi, or low-level chiburi, is executed with the left foot forward. From this chiburi, noto can be more comfortably performed.. Gedan chiburi is more commonly used for advanced techniques.

Kiai - unification of energy

Technically, a kiai is a type of shout emitted while executing a technique. The use of kiai is an important tool for enhancing one's physical technique with powerful spirit, energy and intention. There are several benefits to practicing and developing strong kiai. It allows for two individuals to audibly adjust their timing when practicing basic tachiuchi forms, promotes good health by ensuring natural breathing while training, reduces daily stress and strengthens the diaphragm, stomach and lower back muscles. During a conflict, kiai can focus your energy and provide a means to momentarily disrupt your opponent's concentration. When practicing in large groups, kiai can be used to unite and tighten the focus of the class. However, kiai should not come from only the throat or lungs, but should generate from deep within your diaphragm and expand with all one's power. In Shinkendo, the basic kiai's used are "EI" (EEI), "YA" (YAH), and "TO" (TOH). During partner practice, kiai should be staggered as follows:

| Uchidachi: | *EI* , | | *YA,* | | *TO,* | | *EI,* | | *YA....* |
| Shidachi: | | *YA,* | | *TO,* | | *EI,* | | *YA....* | |

Mesen - placing the focus of the eye

Enzan-no-Me, or "gazing at the distant mountain", is the method of *mesen* (eye placement) used in Shinkendo. When facing an opponent, try to be aware of the opponent's entire body, as well as the terrain and surroundings. In other words, do not focus on any one point, but rather take in all the surroundings equally, in a fashion similar to what happens if one stares at a candle flame. This is what is meant by Enzan-no-Me. "Scatter vision" is a term sometimes used in english to describe this type of gaze. While the eyes should be directed at a given target (or the eyes of the opponent), the primary function of the eye is that of it's peripheral focus. During tameshigiri and tachiuchi, this gaze is useful for judging relative distancing and percieving any obstructions or dangers that may be present. It should be noted that as speed in tachiuchi increases, the range of vision is reduced from 180 degree's to that of a more narrow view (relative to the speed). This phenomena is experienced subconsciously every day by people who drive motor vehicles.

Kamae no Yobikata - Rules for posture nomenclature

When considering the designation (right or left) of kamae, there are two methods that are used:

Those determined by the forward/ leading foot:
•Kamae -   *Jodan, chudan, gedan, kasumi, seigan* and *sei-gedan no kamae*

Those determined by the side the hands are positioned, or where the cut originates:
•Kamae -   *Waki, yoko* and *hasso no kamae*

Kamae - posture

•*Goho no Kamae (kihon)* -   five left side, and five right side
•*Happo no Kamae (jokyu)* -   eight left side, and eight right side

Stances can be divided into two basic types: a "standard" stance consisting of approximately eighteen inches between the feet (a natural stepping distance), and a "deep" stance consisting of approximately thirty inches between the feet. When assuming chudan and jodan no kamae, the standard-stance should be used. Hasso and gedan no kamae also use the standard-stance, or a slightly wider stance. Waki and gedan no kamae use the deep-stance. In all cases, weight balance should be at least 60% over the forward leg, the front foot should point forward, and the back foot should point 45 degree's forward and to the outside.

This provides rapid movement in any direction, and insures maximum range of hip motion.

Waza - Technique

1. *Nukitsuke -* One handed horizontal draw (Goho Battoho, Ipponme)
2. *Tsuki & Hirazuki -* Thrust, blade vertical and horizontal
3. *Migi yokogiri -* Side cut from right to left
4. *Hidari yokogiri -* Side cut from left to right
5. *Migi kesagiri -* Diagonal cut from right to left
6. *Hidari kesagiri -* Diagonal cut from left to right
7. *Migi kiriage -* *(Hidari gyakugesagiri)* Rising diagonal cut from right to left
8. *Hidari kiriage -* *(Migi gyakugesagiri)* Rising diagonal cut from left to right
9. *Shinchokugiri -* Vertical straight cut
10. *Dotangiri -* Vertical straight cut used for test cutting
11. *Nukiuchi -* One handed diagonal cut from left to right
12. *Ura gote -* Reverse under the opponents sword to cut the right wrist
13. *Tsubamegaeshi -* "Sparrow cut". diagonal up/down or down/up cut
14. *Nidan uchi -* Striking twice in rapid succession
15. *Makiuchi nidan -* Performing makiuchi twice in rapid succession
16. *Kasumi uke -* Blocking with the sword in kasumi position
17. *Gyaku gasumi -* Kasumi uke, but with the opposite foot forward
18. *Makiuchi -* Kasumi uke parry, straight cut return - shuffle step only
19. *Kaeshiuchi -* Gyaku kasumi uke parry (opposite of makiuchi), straight cut return - shuffle step only
20. *Kirikaeshi -* Kasumi uke parry, change step and kesagiri return
    a) side to side movement b) forward and back movement
21. *Mikazuki uke -* "Crescent moon block". From a raised position, rotating the blade tip downwards in a crescent path.
22. *Makiosae -* Blade diversion/ parry using left kasumi uke, then stepping forward to right seigan no kamae to control the elbows
23. *Makiotoshi -* Dropping-counter from kasumi uke to chudanzuki
24. *Tachizuke -* Clinging, or "sticky" method of parrying or diversions
25. *Harai uke -* Striking or clinging block
26. *Iwao -* "Rock". Rising block
27. *Seigan uke -* Block from seigan gamae
28. *Mikiri -* Keeping just out of range of an opponent's attack
29. *Jo gedan uke -* High to low block
30. *Sayu uke -* Side to side blocking
31. *Kaeshi -* Reversing cut direction from to return back the same path, as in tsubamegaeshi
32. *Makuri -* Continuous cutting using a 360 degree swing - same cut
33. *Nagashi -* Continuation of one cut to another, as in yoko to kesagiri

素振り
Chapter Seven
Suburi

Stand at migi chudan gamae (right middle stance). Thrusts can be performed to the stomach, chest, neck or face level.

Shuffle forward with the front foot first followed by the back foot. Extend arms forward and thrust from the center; either with the blade vertical or turn the blade 90 degrees counterclockwise if aiming at chest level.

After thrusting, shuffle back with the back foot first, followed by the front (dislodge sword blade), and assume chudan gamae.

SHINCHOKUGIRI

Shinchokugiri is the most basic of all cuts. Start from migi jodan gamae making sure the sword grip and tip are straight above the head.

Shuffle forward with the front foot first followed by the back foot. Swing the sword straight in front of body using an outwards motion. Keep in mind that the cut is done with the sword, not with the hands.

Finish the cut by stopping the with the tip at about knee level (gedan position). Check to see that you have maintained the proper grip.

HIDARI KESAGIRI

Stand from hidari jodan gamae making sure sword grip is above the head. The tip can be straight back or slightly to the right. Start kesagiri by swinging the sword from above the head

Shuffle forward with the front foot first, followed by the back. Swing the sword at a 35 to 40 degree angle. Make sure the sword tip passes through the same swing-path as the grip.

Finish kesagiri by stopping the sword about knee height. Check for proper grip and correct placement of the sword tip. Practice making sure sword does not scoop around in a curved line and watch hasuji (edge-angle).

MIGI KESAGIRI

Stand from migi jodan gamae making sure sword grip is above the head. The tip can be straight back or a bit to the left. Start kesagiri by swinging the sword from above the head.

Shuffle forward with the front foot first, followed by the back. Swing the sword at a 35 to 40 degree angle. Make sure the sword tip passes through the same swing-angle as the grip.

Finish kesagiri by stopping the sword about knee height. Check for proper grip and correct placement of the sword tip. Practice making sure the sword does not scoop around in a curved line and watch hasuji (edge-angle).

HIDARI YOKOGIRI

Start with both feet apart, keeping your balance focused on the left foot. Position the sword at your left side making sure it is parallel to the ground with the blade edge facing directly forward.

Shift your weight to the right foot while swinging the sword horizontally outwards at chest level.

Finish the cut by stopping the sword at the right side of the body. In order to stop the blade correctly, proper grip is essential. Check to see that sword tip and grip are at same height. Balance should now be over the right leg.

MIGI YOKOGIRI

Start with both feet apart, keeping your balance focused on the right foot. Position the sword at your right side, making sure it is parallel to the ground with the blade edge facing directly forward.

Shift your weight to the left foot while swinging the sword outwards at chest level.

Finish the cut by stopping the sword at the left side of the body. In order to stop the blade correctly, proper grip is essential. Check to see that the tip and grip are at the same height. Balance should now be on the left leg.

HIDARI KIRIAGE

Start from right foot forward, hidari waki gamae. Make sure the sword tip is not too far behind back right foot. Sword tip should be about 12 inches to the right of the right foot and not behind.

Shuffle forward with the front foot while cutting upwards at a 35 or 40 degree angle.

Finish kiriage by stopping the blade so the grip does not pass behind the head. Balance should not become too high, and both feet should be planted firmly on the ground.

MIGI KIRIAGE

Start from left foot forward, migi waki gamae. Make sure the sword tip is not too far behind the back-left leg. Sword tip should be about 12 inches to the left of the left foot and not behind.

Shuffle forward with the front foot while cutting upwards at a 35 or 40 degree angle.

Finish kiriage by stopping the blade so the grip does not pass behind the head. Balance should not become too high, and both feet should be planted firmly on the ground.

抜刀法

Chapter Eight
Battoho

Battoho explores the five basic methods of drawing the Japanese sword. These five ways (goho) consist of *katate nukitsuke* (side cut draw), migikesa (right diagonal draw), kiriage (rising diagonal draw & cut), *nukiuchi* (one-handed left diagonal draw), and *hineri* (draw and thrust). Drawing the sword effectively in any direction is possible when these five draws are combined with proper ashisabaki (footwork), taisabaki (body movement), and *kaiten dosa* (turning). Battoho should be studied continuously by beginning, intermediate, and advanced students. In advanced variations, battoho can be practiced as partnered tachiuchi or applied to tameshigiri. Kata include: *Goho Battoho Kihon Ichi* (basic), *Goho Battoho Kihon Ni* (advanced), *Santengiri, Shiho, Shiho Ura, Hangetsu, Mangetsu, Hangetsugaeshi, Mangetsugaeshi, Gotengiri,* and *Goho-gogyo.*

Goho Battoho Kihon Ichi

Kihon Ichi is the most basic of the Battoho series. When you are performing it, count each step slowly and make sure that all cuts and kamae are exact. Because Kihon Ichi is a basic kata, the makuri, kaeshi and nagashi techniques are not incorporated. Stop the sword at the end of each cut (tome), then assume the next kamae. When performing battoho, chiburi and noto, *always* do so carefully. If practicing with a bokuto or iaito, the same care and precision should be adhered to as that used when working with a *shinken* (live blade). Drawing and sheathing can be very dangerous; following this simple rule will greatly assist in the transition to using a real sword.

五法抜刀法　　基本一
一本目

GOHO BATTOHO KIHON ICHI:

IPPONME

Ipponme is the first kata of the Goho Battoho Kihon Ichi set. Composed of two cuts, Ipponme begins with katate nukitsuke (one handed side cut draw) followed by hidari kesagiri, and ending with jodan chiburi, noto.

#1 *Kiotsuke*
Stand at ready position.

#2 *Count one*
Step forward with right foot, begin katate nukitsuke (side cut draw with one hand).

#5 Finish stepping forward with left foot, hidari kesagiri.

#6 Finish hidari kesagiri.

#3 Right foot steps forward, complet katate nukitsuke.

#4 *Count two*
Begin stepping forward with left foot, jodan position.

#7 *Count three*
Right foot steps forward, migi chudan gamae.

#8 *Count four*
Jodan chiburi ichi (1).

#9 Jodan chiburi ni (2).   **#10** Jodan chiburi san (3).

#13 Noto.   **#14** Noto - finishing.

#11 *Count five*
Noto (re-sheath).

#12 Noto.

#15 Left foot steps forward, feet
together. Slide right hand
forward, cover the end of the
sword hilt.

#16 *Kiotsuke*
Finishing position.

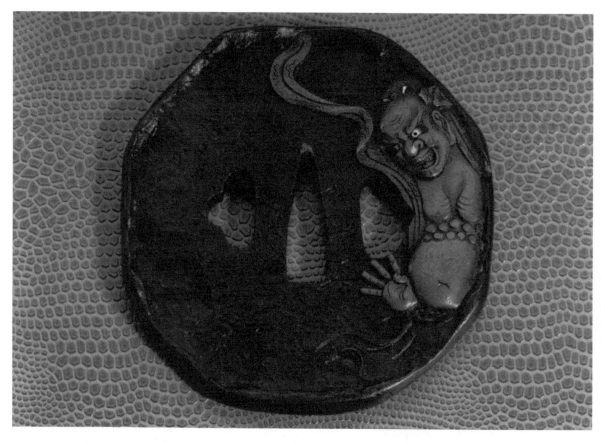

Toshimitsu

五法抜刀法　基本一
二本目

GOHO BATTO HO KIHON ICHI:
NIHONME

Nihonme is the second kata of the Goho Battoho Kihon Ichi set. Composed of two cuts, nihonme begins with migi kesagiri (right diagonal cut), followed by hidari kesagiri (left diagonal cut), and ending with jodan chiburi, noto.

#1 *Kiotsuke*
Stand at ready position.

#2 *Count one*
Right foot steps forward, one-handed draw to jodan-gamae.

#5 Migi kesagiri.

#6 Finish migi kesagiri.

#3 One handed migi jodan-gamae.   **#4** Raise left hand and assume two-handed migi jodan-gamae.

#7 *Count two*
Raise sword to jodan-gamae.

#8 Left foot steps forward, jodan position.

#9 Left foot steps forward, hidari kesagiri.

#10 Finish hidari kesagiri.

#13 Jodan chiburi ni (2).

#14 Jodan chiburi san (3).

#11 *Count three*
Right foot steps forward, migi chudan gamae.

#12 *Count four*
Jodan chiburi ichi (1).

#15 *Count five*
Noto (sheath).

#16 *Kiotsuke*
Left foot steps forward.
Finishing position.

Kyo Sukashi

五法抜刀法　　基本一
三本目

GOHO BATTOHO KIHON ICHI:
SANBONME

Sanbonme is the third kata of the Goho Battoho Kihon Ichi set. Composed of two cuts, sanbonme begins with katate kiriage (one handed rising diagonal cut), followed by hidari kesagiri (left diagonal cut), and ending with chudan chiburi, noto.

#1 *Kiotsuke*
Stand at ready position.

#2 *Count one*
Right foot steps forward, migi katate kiriage (one hand diagonal rising cut draw).

#5 Left foot steps forward, hidari kesagiri.

#6 Finish hidari kesagiri.

#3 Finish kiriage.

#4 *Count two*
Left foot steps forward, jodan
position.

#7 *Count three*
Right foot steps forward, migi
chudan gamae.

#8 *Count four*
Chudan chiburi.

#9 *Count five*
Noto (re-sheath).

#10 Noto.

#11 Left foot steps forward, feet together. Slide right hand forward, cover top of sword hilt.

#12 *Kiotsuke*
Finishing position.

Seigan no Kamae

Sakura Fubuki
(Cherry Blossom)

五法抜刀法　基本一
四本目

GOHO BATTOHO KIHON ICHI:
YONHONME

Yonhonme is the forth kata of the Goho Battoho Kihon Ichi set. Composed of two cuts, yonhonme begins with hidari nukiuchi (one handed left diagonal cut, followed by migi kesagiri, and ending with chudan chiburi, noto.

#1 *Kiotsuke*
Stand at ready position.

#2 *Count one*
Left foot steps forward, begin nukiuchi (one hand overhead draw and cut).

#5 Finish one hand hidari kesagiri.

#6 *Count two*
Right foot steps forward, raise sword to jodan position.

#3 One handed jodan gamae.

#4 Katate hidari kesagiri (one hand left diagonal cut).

#7 Right foot steps forward, migi kesagiri.

#8 Finish migi kesagiri.

#9 *Count three*
Shuffle forward, migi
chudan gamae.

#10 *Count four*
Chudan chiburi.

#13 Left foot steps forward, feet
together. Slide right hand
forward, cover top of sword hilt.

#14 *Kiotsuke*
Finishing position.

#11 *Count five*
Noto (re-sheath).

#12 Noto.

Nobuie

五法抜刀法　　基本一
五本目

GOHO BATTOHO KIHON ICHI:
GOHONME

Gohonme is the fifth kata of the Goho Battoho Kihon Ichi set. Composed of two cuts, gohonme begins with hineri (one hand draw to thrust position), and hirazuki (one hand thrust) followed by migi kesagiri (right diagonal cut), and ending with chudan chiburi, noto.

#1 *Kiotsuke*
Stand at ready position.

#2 *Count one*
Right foot steps back, hineri (draw sword to thrust position).

#5 Hirazuki (one hand thrust).

#6 Pull sword back.

#3 Thrust position.

#4 (Reverse view of #3 *Kamae*).

#7 *Count two*
Raise sword to hidari jodan gamae.

#8 Right foot steps forward, migi kesagiri (right diagonal cut).

#9 Finish migi kesagiri.

#10 *Count three*
Shuffle forward, migi chudan gamae.

#13 Noto.

#14 Left foot steps forward, feet together. Slide right hand forward, cover top of sword hilt.

#11 *Count four*
Chudan chiburi.

#12 *Count five*
Noto (re-sheath).

#15 *Kiotsuke*
Finishing position.

Chapter Nine
Shinkendo Tanrengata

The Shinkendo Tanren gata is a set consisting of ten kata. They include:

1. Happogiri: Basic eight cuts - tsuki, hidari yokogiri, migi kiriage, hidari kesagiri, migi yokogiri, hidari kiriage, migi kesagiri and dotangiri (straight center cut). These are put together in one kata and practiced.

2. Happogiri ura: This incorporates the basic eight ways to cut with larger wider foot move ments. Right turn movement and left turn movements are involved.

3. Shoden-no-kata: This is a twelve count kata which includes two sets of 3-cut combina tions, and ending with chiburi, noto.

4. Kagami-ishi usen: beginning with migi yoko nukitsuki batto, shuffle step, regular step and turn. Side step and stepping forward and back. These footwork are the basics of this kata.

5. Kagami-ishi sasen: This is the mirror technique of Kagami-ishi usen.

These first five kata form Shinkendo Tanrengata's basics and as such are detailed in the following technical section. They should be practiced slowly and precisely. The main point is to practice and improve, ashisabaki (footwork), taisabaki (body movement), *kensabaki* (sword swings), *jyushin no ido* (balance shifting), shuffle stepping, walking stepping, and turning. Testcutting can be practiced safely once the body has memorized these basic principles. Improvements in these areas will crossover and be clearly seen in other forms and tachiuchi.

6. Chuden sei: This is first practiced with a twelve count, but some counts include two or three movement. With this practice body movements will become smoother and faster.

7. Chuden do: This is done cutting 1 target 3 times first on the right then left side, then cutting 3 times on 3 targets.

8. Jugo: This begins as a Santengiri with a kesa/ yokogiri combination, a tsubamegaeshi combination and a three point cutting combination. This is done on both sides.

9. Jugo shiho: This kata is Jugo performed in four directions, and focuses on balance and combination cuts.

10. Goho hoen: A combination of techniques found in the first 9 kata. Involves cutting 4 direction, 8 direction, left turn, right turn, draw and sheath. Additionally the 4 direction uses pivoting, one step, and two step variations. This technique variation can be repeatedly, without stopping.

Katas 6 through 10 should be practiced slowly and precisely at first, but later can be practiced naturally, fast and with power.

八方斬り

HAPPOGIRI

Happogiri consists of the eight basic cuts used in Shinkendo. These cuts include migi and hidari kesagiri (right and left diagonal cut), migi and hidari kiriage (right and left rising diagonal cut), migi and hidari yokogiri (right and left side cut), hirazuki (thrust) and dotangiri (straight cut). When practicing Happogiri, concentrate on precise cuts and footwork. Make sure that cutting angle, and blade edge angle (hasuji) are exact.

#1 *Kiotsuke*
Stand at ready position.

#2 *Kamae*
Right foot steps forward, migi chudan-gamae.

#3 *Count one*
Shuffle forward, hirazuki (thrust, turning sword 90 degrees counter-clockwise).

#7 Finish hidari yokogiri (left side cut).

#8 *Count three*
Left foot steps forward, ready position for kiriage.

#9 Shuffle forward, migi kiriage (right rising diagonal cut).

#4 Shuffle back, return to chudan-gamae.

#5 *Count two* Right foot steps back, ready position for hidari yokogiri (left side cut).

#6 Right foot steps sideways, hidari yokogiri.

#10 Finish migi kiriage.

#11 *Count four* Bring sword to hidari jodan-gamae.

#12 Shuffle back, hidari kesagiri (left diagonal cut).

#13 Finish hidari kesagiri.

#14 *Count five* Left foot steps back, ready for migi yokogiri.

#15 Left foot steps sideways, migi yokogiri (right side cut).

#19 Finish hidari kiriage.

#20 *Count seven* Migi jodan gamae.

#21 Shuffle back, migi kesagiri.

#16 Finish migi yokogiri (right side cut).

#17 *Count six* Right foot steps forward, ready for hidari kiriage.

#18 Shuffle forward, hidari kiriage (left rising diagonal cut).

#22 Migi kesagiri, nagashi.

#23 Raise sword to jodan position, while stepping back with right foot.

#24 *Count eight* Ready for dotangiri.

#25 Dotangiri.   **#26** Dotangiri.   **#27** Right foot steps forward, migi chudan gamae. Finishing position.

Tachiaigoshi

Shigure-Tei (Tea House in Kyoto)

初 伝 の 型

SHODEN NO KATA

Through practicing Shoden no kata, body movement becomes more relaxed and natural. Shoden no kata should first be practiced using twelve counts - as described in this book. In addition to using twelve counts, advanced students should practice Shoden no kata using four counts, and finally without a count. Begining students should focus on executing exact cuts and proper footwork, while more advanced students should incorporate flexability and natural movement into the kata.

#1 *Kiotsuke*
Stand at ready position.

#2 *Yoi*
Kneel down.

#3 *Count one*
Stand up. Open koiguchi.

#7 Raise sword to hidari jodan gamae.

#8 *Count four*
Left foot steps back then sideways, migi kesagiri (right diagonal cut).

#9 Finish migi kesagiri.

#4 *Count two*
Right foot steps sideways, while drawing sword.

#5 *Count three*
Bring left foot together with the right.

#6 Left foot steps forward, raise sword to chudan gamae.

#10 *Count five*
Bring right foot together with left, ready yokogiri.

#11 Right foot steps forward, hidari yokogiri (left side cut).

#12 Hidari yokogiri finish.

#13 Raise sword to jodan gamae (nagashi).

#14 *Count six* Right foot steps back to jodan position.

#15 Right foot steps sideways, hidari kesagiri (left diagonal cut).

#19 *Count eight* Kneeling position, waki gamae.

#20 Hidari kiriage from kneeling position, twisting hips.

#21 Finish hidari kiriage.

#16 Finish hidari kesagiri.

#17 *Count seven* Left foot steps back to kneeling position while raising sword to kasumi gamae.

#18 Kasumi gamae from kneeling position.

#22 *Count nine* Stand up, while bringing sword to thrust position.

#23 Left foot steps forward, tsuki (thrust).

#24 *Count ten* Raise sword to kasumi gamae.

#25 Left foot steps back, raise sword to jodan position.

#26 Left foot steps sideways, ready for dotangiri.

#27 Dotangiri.

#31 Jodan chiburi ni (2).

#32 Jodan chiburi (from ni to san).

#33 Jodan chiburi san (3).

104

#28 Finish dotangiri.

#29 *Count eleven*
Bring left foot together
with right foot, raise
sword to chudan
position.

#30 Left foot steps
back, jodan chiburi
ichi (1).

#34 *Count twelve*
Left foot steps
forward, feet together.

#35 Right foot step
back.

#36 Noto (sheath).

#37 Noto.

#38 Right foot steps forward, feet together.

#39 Bring right hand to top of sword hilt.

#40 *Kiotsuke*
Finishing position.

鏡石　　右旋

KAGAMI-ISHI
USEN

Kagami-ishi usen (clockwise) and sasen (counter-clockwise) are basic kata which incorporate fundamental concepts of Shinkendo swordsmanship. Practice the Kagami-ishi kata slowly and count by count in order to maintain proper balance and develop strong posture. After each cut, pause and come to an exact kamae before continuing to the next count.

#1 *Kiotsuke*
Starting position.

#2 *Count one*
Right foot steps forward,
nukitsuke (one handed
side cut draw).

#5 *Count two*
Left foot steps forward, migi
kiriage (right rising diagonal cut).

#6 Finish kiriage.

#3 Finish nukitsuke.

#4 Ready for count two.
Lower sword to waki gamae.

#7 Ready for count three.
Bring sword to hidari jodan
gamae.

#8 *Count three*
Right foot steps forward, migi
kesagiri (right diagonal cut).

#9 Finish migi kesagiri.

#10 *Count four*
Left foot steps forward, pivot clockwise raising sword to kasumi gamae.

#13 Right foot steps back, hidari kesagiri (left diagonal cut).

#14 Finish hidari kesagiri.

#11 Kasumi gamae.

#12 Right foot steps back to jodan position.

#15 Ready for count five. Bring sword to migi waki gamae, ready for migi kiriage (right rising diagonal cut).

#16 *Count five*
Shuffle forward, migi kiriage.

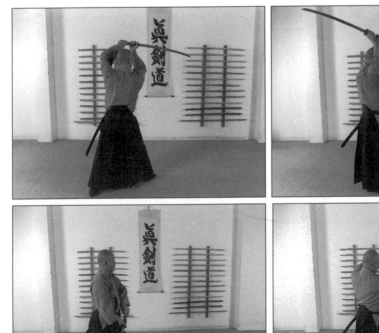

#17 Finish migi kiriage.

#18 Ready for count six. Bring sword to hidari jodan gamae.

#21 *Count seven*
Left foot steps forward, pivot clockwise raising sword to kasumi gamae.

#22 Kasumi gamae.

#19 *Count six*
Right foot steps forward,
migi kesagiri (right diagonal
cut).

#20 Finish migi kesagiri.

#23 Right foot steps back to
jodan position.

#24 Right foot steps back,
hidari kesagiri (left diagonal cut).

#25 Finish hidari kesagiri.

#26 Ready for count eight. Left foot steps back, ready for migi yokogiri (right side cut).

#29 Ready for count nine. Lower sword to waki gamae, right foot steps forward.

#30 *Count nine* Shuffle forward, hidari kiriage (left rising diagonal cut).

#27 *Count eight*
Left foot steps sideways,
migi yokogiri.

#28 Finish migi yokogiri.

#31 Finish hidari kiriage.

#32 Ready for count ten.
Bring sword to jodan gamae.

#33 *Count ten*
Right foot steps back, hidari kesa-giri (left diagonal cut).

#34 Finish hidari kesagiri.

#37 Right foot steps forward, feet together.

#38 *Kiotsuke*
Finishing position.

#35 Shuffle back, gedan chiburi.   **#36** Noto (sheath).

Nami ni Hana
(Wave and Flower)

鏡石　　左旋

KAGAMI-ISHI
SASEN

Kagami-ishi sasen (counter-clockwise) is the second of the two Kagami-ishi kata. You will notice that all the techniques are the same as in Kagami-ishi usen, but executed from the opposite side, and with a different draw.

#1 *Kiotsuke*
Stand at ready position.

#2 *Count one*
Right foot steps forward, one
hand draw raising sword to
jodan gamae.

#5 Migi kesagiri (right
diagonal cut).

#6 Finish migi kesagiri.

#3 Raise sword to migi jodan position.

#4 Migi jodan gamae.

#7 Ready for count two. Bring sword to hidari waki gamae.

#8 *Count two*
Shuffle forward, hidari kiriage (left rising diagonal cut).

#9 Finish hidari kiriage.

#10 Ready for count three.
Bring sword to migi jodan gamae.

#13 *Count four*
Right foot steps forward,
pivot counterclockwise raising
sword to kasumi gamae.

#14 Kasumi gamae.

#11 *Count three*
Left foot steps forward,
hidari kesagiri (left diagonal
cut).

#12 Finish hidari kesagiri.

#15 Bring sword to hidari
jodan gamae.

#16 Left foot steps back, migi
kesagiri (right diagonal cut).

#17 Finish migi kesagiri.

#18 Ready for count five. Bring sword to hidari waki gamae.

#21 Finish hidari kiriage.

#22 Ready for count six. Bring sword to migi jodan gamae.

#19 *Count five*
Right foot shuffles forward begin hidari kiriage (left rising diagonal cut).

#20 Hidari kiriage.

#23 *Count six*
Left foot steps forward, hidari kesagiri (left diagonal cut).

#24 Finish hidari kesagiri.

#25 *Count seven*
Right foot steps forward, pivot counter clockwise raising sword to kasumi gamae.

#26 Kasumi gamae.

#29 Finish migi kesagiri.

#30 Ready for count eight. Right foot steps back, ready for hidari yokogiri (left side cut).

#27 Bring sword to hidari jodan gamae.

#28 Left foot steps back, migi kesagiri (right diagonal cut).

#31 *Count eight*
Right foot steps sideways, hidari yokogiri (left side cut).

#32 Finish hidari yokogiri.

#33 Ready for count nine.
Lower sword to waki gamae, left
foot steps forward.

#34 *Count nine*
Shuffle forward, migi kiriage
(right rising diagonal cut).

#37 *Count ten*
Left foot steps back, migi
kesagiri (right diagonal cut).

#38 Finish migi kesagiri.
Shuffle forward to chudan
gamae.

#35 Finish migi kiriage.

#36 Ready for count ten. Bring sword to hidari jodan gamae.

#39 Chudan chiburi.

#40 Noto (sheath).

129

#41 Noto.

#42 Left foot steps forward, feet together.

#43 *Kiotsuke*
Finishing position.

Mitsudomoe Ko Shoami

Torii no Kamae Uke

Shomen Uchi

太刀打
Chapter Ten
Tachiuchi

Tachiuchi Practice

It is important for some form of tachiuchi to be included in the study of martial arts so that a student may understand how to adjust to a moving target. Kata and tameshigiri teach one how to cut stationary targets, and while this practice is important, only tachiuchi emphasizes a dynamic interplay between moving targets.

Six fundamental elements of tachiuchi

- Fighting strategy (*heiho*)
- Power (*chikara*)
- Rhythm (*hyoshi*)
- Distance (*ma-ai*)
- Speed (*sokudo*)
- Energy (*tanryoku*)

These elements must be explored deeply to understand *riai* (the application of an art). A student must constantly be aware of the distance between themselves and that of their opponent.

All the movements in basic tachiuchi are pre-arranged, allowing students to focus on harmonizing with their opponents movements instead of simply over-coming them. This type of tachiuchi is sometimes called "promise tachiuchi", in reference to the trust required between practitioners. It would be inappropriate for a more advanced student to use fast, powerful techniques on a less advanced student.

In addition to one's own ability, there are other factors that should be considered when practicing tachiuchi. One important element of tachiuchi is the capability to adjust to your partner's ability level. Besides being necessary for safe practice, these adjustments can also be used to "lead" your partner to improved technique and/or mental attitude. If your partner lacks energy (*tanryoku*), it is possible to increase their energy through vigorous tachiuchi. The influence of your own higher-level of energy can induce your partner to raise their energy to rival it.

When teaching or observing tachiuchi, the level of the students can be judged by their ability to effectively blend with partners of various skill levels. For instance, if an ideal value of 10 is given to the ability of a pair of practitioners to train together harmoniously, several different ratios of skill levels could be used to reach that value. For example if one person's skill level is two then the other person, usually the more advanced practitioner, should adjust their level to be eight in order for them to train together with the greatest amount of safety and harmony. In the case of advanced students, both would generally practice at skill levels of five to reach the ideal of 10.

Defender =   1 | 2 | 3 | 4 | 5 | 6 | 7 | 8 | 9
Attacker =   9 | 8 | 7 | 6 | 5 | 4 | 3 | 2 | 1

Regardless of the numeric combination - or, levels of ability - the end result should be that of proper adjustment between training partners. For two practitioners to train at a level of three (equaling a total level of six) would be counterproductive. An instructor should consider this principle when pairing up students.

During practice, students should focus on elements of tachiuchi that pertain to their level of ability (*safe practice and good quality bokken should always be used*) :

Beginning Students:
   •Practice tachiuchi slowly and precisely in order to ensure proper techique, distance, and timing.
   •Try to recognize and mimic the good techniques of more advanced students.

Intermediate Students:
   •As the students begin to advance, speed and power can be increased.
   •Variations of techniques can be learned by experimenting with distance and timing.

Advanced Students:
   •The sword tactics and strategies of *go-ju, kan-kyu* and *kyo-jitsu* should be studied and practiced (see below).
   •When your partner moves back, move forward. If your partner moves forward, avoid the attack by moving to one side.
   •Avoid making any unnecessary movements. When practicing tachiuchi, one should be as efficient with movement as possible. Taking extra steps, stutter steps, or moving too dramatically can lead to inefficient technique and leave openings for attack. Moving the smallest amount necessary to avoid an attack is called "*mikiri*". Clear judgement of mikiri is critical in advanced tachiuchi.

Philosophical and tactical principles are found even in the early stages of training. Two examples of these principles are: "*go, ju, ryu, ki, rei*" and "*ju yoku go o seishi - go yoku ju o tatsu, hike ba ose - ose ba maware*" . In English, the former means "hard, soft, liquid, energy, inherited cognizance/ soul", while the latter translates as "soft controls hard - hard cuts soft", and "If pulled, push - If pushed, turn". Shinkendo incorporates these qualities in its techniques. A deep understanding of these principles necessitates instruction by a qualified instructor..

The main goal of tachiuchi in Shinkendo is not that of defeating your partner, but rather the mutual refinement of technique. However, it should be understood that through diligent study, the 6 elements can be slightly altered to disrupt the flow and balance of the tachiuchi. This is an advanced concept usually reserved for application in combat or self-defense, and should not be practiced without proper supervision.

Go-Ju, Kan-Kyu, Kyo-Jitsu

Shinkendo Tachiuchi applies the concepts of go (hard) ju (soft), kan (slow) kyu (fast) and kyo (negative/fake) jitsu (true/real).

The concept of go-ju is one of the first strategic elements to which students are introduced. The utilization of hard or strong techniques, combined with soft or flowing techniques is fundamental to tachiuchi. Go-ju uses the elements of power and energy.

When practicing kan, use slower, precise movements with strong intention. When using faster movements, or kyu, your mind should remain calm, flexible and focused. kan-kyu is directly related to the timing, speed and rhythm of a tachiuchi.

Kyo-Jitsu can be seen clearly in other arts, such as modern boxing. Kyo is a jab, or feint motion used to distract, weaken or create openings in the opponent. It also allows the attacker to quickly defend against a possible counter-strike, where as a fully committed strike would be too difficult to recover from. Jitsu is used once an opening has been established to finish the opponent. The same principles are applied to sword tachiuchi. Strategy, distance, go-ju and kan-kyu are combined with the above principle to advance the study of kyo-jitsu.

During pre-arranged tachiuchi, there is a set offense and defense, but during a real battle, this is not the case. By studying the concepts of go-ju, kan-kyu and kyo-jitsu, you will begin to develop strong tachiuchi.

There are two basic scenarios in tachiuchi: those that include a counter-attack or riposte -and those that do not. When the defender performs a counter-attack, the terms *uchidachi* (initiate) and *shidachi* (receive & retaliate) are used. Alternately, tachiuchi that do not incorporate a counter-attack by the defender use the terms *uchite* (strike) and *ukete* (receive). Juppon-dachi is an example of the uchidachi/shidachi relationship, while Ryusui demonstrates an uchite/ukete interaction.

Rokudo (Basic six) Tachiuchi

Rokudo is usually the first tachiuchi taught, and as such warrants a brief overview. While this tachiuchi consists of six sections, the first four sections are considered basic, and are often performed solo at first by a new student. In sections 1-4, the partners face each other and mirror one another's movements. The tips of the swords should not meet, and the feeling, angles and timing of the cuts should match exactly. The advanced person must check the beginner's hasuji (edge angle), tachisuji (cutting line), position of tome (stopping) and ma-ai (distance). Practice should be slow and precise.

- Basic side starts in migi chudan-gamae, advanced in migi hasso-gamae
- Use four counts stepping forward (basic side), then four counts stepping back (basic side)
- The object of this tachiuchi is to match the angle and speed of your partner
- Kiai "Ei, Yah, Toh" should be emphasized during tachiuchi

1) *Ipponme* - Ichi no tachi (straight cut)

2) *Nihonme* - Ichi no tachi kesa (diagonal cut).

3) *Sanbonme* - Makuri (kesa makuri).

4) *Yonhonme* - Tsubamegaeshi (kesagiri/kiriage).

5) *Gohonme* - Ichi no tachi kasumi (center strike/kiri kaeshi)
   Shidachi drops to gedan to leave an opening. Uchidachi attacks immediately using a straight cut. Shidachi blocks with kasumi and returns with a straight cut.

6) *Ropponme* - Ichi no tachi kesa kasumi (kesagiri/ kiri kaeshi/ center strike return) Shidachi drops to gedan to leave an opening. Uchidachi attacks immediately using kesa giri. Shidachi blocks with a steep kasumi and returns with a straight cut.

Kasumi Uke

Uchikomi
(Shomen Uchi)

RYUSUI
PART ONE

Ryusui is a basic tachiuchi which focuses on shuffling and stepping practice. Because the defending side of the tachiuchi does not counter attack, the name ukete has been used (instead of shidachi), and the attacking side has been named uchite (instead of uchidachi). Ryusui is usually performed in sequence with a pause in between each set, but for the purpose of this book, Ryusui has been broken down into three sets of four techniques. After the final set is performed, the defending side takes one step back to hasso gamae becoming uchite and the attacking side takes migi seigan gamae becoming ukete. From this position, Ryusui is performed again - this time with roles reversed. Ryusui san (3) is the third and final part of the Ryusui tachiuchi. When attacking, uchite should use strong kiai. This aids in maintaining good rhythm and helps the tachiuchi "flow".

#1 *Kiotsuke*
Bow to your partner, and assume ready position.

#2 *Kamae*
Uchite: Right foot steps back, drawing sword to migi hasso gamae.

Ukete: Right foot steps forward, drawing sword to migi seigan gamae.

#5 *Count two*
Uchite: Shuffle forward, chudanzuki (middle thrust).

Ukete: Shuffle back, seigedan uke.

#6
Uchite: Pull sword back to chudan gamae.

Ukete: Migi seigedan gamae.

#3 *Count one*

Uchite: Right foot steps forward, shomen uchi (straight cut).

Ukete: Shuffle back, kasumi uke.

#4

Uchite: Pull sword back to chudan gamae.

Ukete: Ready for gedan uke.

#7 *Count three*

Uchite: Shuffle forward, jodanzuki (upper thrust).

Ukete: Shuffle back, migi seigan uke (block to the left).

#8

Uchite: Pull sword back to chudan gamae.

Ukete: Migi gyaku seigan gamae (right foot forward, sword tip to the left).

#9 Count four

Uchite: Left foot steps forward, jodanzuki (upper thrust).

Ukete: Right foot steps back, hidari seigan uke (block to the right).

#10

Uchite: Raise sword to jodan gamae.

Ukete: Hidari seigan gamae.

流水

RYUSUI
PART TWO

#1

Uchite: Start from hidari jodan gamae.

Ukete: Start from hidari seigan gamae.

#2 Count one

Uchite: Right foot steps forward, shomen uchi (straight cut).

Ukete: Shuffle back, kasumi uke.

#5

Uchite: Pull sword back to chudan gamae.

Ukete: Migi seigedan gamae.

#6 *Count three*

Uchite: Shuffle forward, jodanzuki (upper thrust).

Ukete: Shuffle back, migi seigan uke (block to the left).

#3

Uchite: Pull sword back to chudan gamae.

Ukete: Hidari dai jodan gamae (raise sword vertically above your head).

#4 *Count two*

Uchite: Shuffle forward, chudanzuki (middle thrust).

Ukete: Left foot step back, mikazuki uke.

#7

Uchite: Pull sword back to chudan gamae.

Ukete: Bring sword to migi gyaku seigan gamae (right foot forward, sword tip to the left).

#8 *Count four*

Uchite: Left foot steps forward, jodanzuki (upper thrust).

Ukete: Right foot steps back, hidari seigan uke (block to the right).

Seigan Uke

Uchikomi

流水

RYUSUI
PART THREE

147

#1

Uchite: Start from hidari jodan gamae.

Ukete: Start from hidari seigan gamae.

#2 *Count one*

Uchite: Right foot steps forward, shomen uchi (straight cut).

Ukete: Shuffle back, kasumi uke.

#5

Uchite: Pull sword back to chudan gamae.

Ukete: Hidari seigedan gamae.

#6 *Count three*

Uchite: Left foot steps forward, jodanzuki (upper thrust).

Ukete: Shuffle back, hidari seigan uke (block to the right).

#3

Uchite: Pull sword back to chudan gamae.

Ukete: Hidari kasumi gamae.

#4 *Count two*

Uchite: Shuffle forward, chudanzuki (middle thrust).

Ukete: Shuffle back, seigedan uke.

#7

Uchite: Pull sword back to chudan gamae.

Ukete: Hidari gyaku seigedan gamae (left foot forward gedan gamae, tip to the right).

#8 *Count four*

Uchite: Right foot steps forward, jodanzuki (upper thrust).

Ukete: Left foot step back, migi seigan uke (block to the left).

Jodan no Kamae　　　　　　Seigan no Kamae

十本太刀

JUPPON-DACHI

Juppon-dachi is an intermediate to advanced tachiuchi sparring exercise that focuses on developing shidachi, or the defending side. The techniques practiced by shidachi in Juppon-dachi include: kirikaeshi, makiuchi, koteuchi, and makiosae. Practice slowly and carefuly, count by count. When begining, focus not on speed and power, but concentrate more on timing, distance and proper technique.

Shidachi	**Uchidachi**
1. Migi Kirikaeshi	1. Uchikomi
2. Migi Makiuchi	2. Uchikomi
3. Hidari Kirikaeshi	3. Uchikomi
4. Hidari Makiuchi	4. Uchikomi
5. Migi Kirikaeshi	5. Uchikomi
6. Gyaku Seigan Uke	6. Uragote
7. Sayu Uke	7. Nidanzuki
8. Hidari Kirikaeshi	8. Uchikomi
9. Makiosae	9. Uchikomi
10. Migi Makiuchi	10. Uchikomi

#1 *Kamae*

Uchidachi: Start from left foot forward migi hasso gamae.

Shidachi: Start from hidari seigan gamae.

#2 *Count one* - *Kirikaeshi*

Uchidachi: Right foot steps forward, shomen uchi (straight cut).

Shidachi: Right foot steps diagonally forward, kasumi uke.

#5 *Count two* - *Makiuchi*

Uchidachi: Right foot steps back to hidari jodan gamae.

Shidachi: Migi seigan gamae.

#6

Uchidachi: Right foot steps forward, shomen uchi (straight cut).

Shidachi: Shuffle diagonally back, kasumi uke.

#3

Uchidachi: Continue shomen uchi.

Shidachi: Left foot follows, migi kesagiri.

#4

Uchidachi: Shuffle back to migi chudan gamae (adjust to shidachi).

Shidachi: Migi seigan gamae.

#7

Uchidachi: Continue shomen uchi.

Shidachi: From kasumi uke, raise sword to jodan gamae.

#8

Uchidachi: Finish shomen uchi.

Shidachi: Shuffle forward, shomen uchi.

#9
Uchidachi: Right foot step s back to hidari chudan gamae.

Shidachi: Shuffle back to migi seigan gamae.

#10 ***Count three*** - *Kirikaeshi*
Uchidachi: Raise sword to hidari jodan gamae.

Shidachi: Migi seigan gamae.

#13
Uchidachi: Finish shomen uchi.

Shidachi: Hidari kesagiri.

#14
Uchidachi: Shuffle back to migi chudan gamae (adjust to shidachi).
Shidachi: Shuffle back to hidari seigan gamae.

#11
Uchidachi: Right foot steps forward, shomen uchi (straight cut).

Shidachi: Left foot steps diagonally forward, kasumi uke.

#12
Uchidachi: Continue shomen uchi.

Shidachi: Right foot follows, bring sword to hidari jodan gamae.

#15 *Count four* - *Makiuchi*
Uchidachi: Right foot steps back to hidari jodan gamae.

Shidachi: Hidari seigan gamae.

#16
Uchidachi: Right foot steps forward, shomen uchi (straight cut).

Shidachi: Shuffle diagonally back, kasumi uke.

#17

Uchidachi: Continue shomen uchi.

Shidachi: Raise sword to hidari jodan gamae.

#18

Uchidachi: Finish shomen uchi (straight cut).

Shidachi: Shuffle forward, shomen uchi.

#21

Uchidachi: Right foot steps forward, shomen uchi (straight cut).

Shidachi: Right foot steps diagonally forward, kasumi uke.

#22

Uchidachi: Continue shomen uchi.

Shidachi: Left foot follows, migi kesagiri.

#19

Uchidachi: Raise sword to migi chudan gamae.

Shidachi: Hidari seigan gamae.

#20 *Count five - Kirikaeshi*

Uchidachi: Right foot steps back to hidari jodan gamae.

Shidachi: Hidari seigan gamae.

#23

Uchidachi: Adjust to shidachi, migi seigan uke (block to the left).

Shidachi: Continue migi kesagiri.

#24 *Count six - Gyaku seigan uke*

Uchidachi: Migi chudan gamae.

Shidachi: Migi seigan gamae.

#25

Uchidachi: Uragote
(reverse wrist strike).

Shidachi: Gyaku seigan uke
(block to the right).

#26

Uchidachi: Right steps back, hidari
seigan uke (block to the right).

Shidachi: Left foot steps forward,
jodanzuki (upper thrust).

#29

Uchidachi: Right foot steps forward, jodanzuki (upper thrust).

Shidachi: Left foot steps back,
migi seigan uke (block to the left).

#30 *Count eight* - *Kirikaeshi*

Uchidachi: Raise sword to jodan
gamae.

Shidachi: Migi seigan gamae.

#27 *Count seven* - *Sayu uke*
Uchidachi: Shuffle forward, jodanzuki (upper thrust).

Shidachi: Shuffle back, hidari seigan uke (block to the right).

#28
Uchidachi: Pull sword back to chudan gamae.

Shidachi: Hidari gyaku seigan gamae (left foot forward, sword tip to the right).

#31
Uchidachi: Shuffle forward, shomen uchi (straight cut).

Shidachi: Left foot steps diagonally forward, kasumi uke.

#32
Uchidachi: Finish shomen uchi.

Shidachi: Right foot follows, hidari kesa giri.

#33

Uchidachi: Migi chudan gamae.

Shidachi: Hidari seigan gamae.

#34 *Count nine* - *Makiosae*

Uchidachi: Right foot steps back to hidari jodan gamae.

Shidachi: Hidari seigan gamae.

#37

Uchidachi: Finish shomen uchi, shuffle back as shidachi advances.

Shidachi: From migi seigan gamae, control uchidachi's elbows.

#38 *Count ten* - *Makiuchi*

Uchidachi: Right foot steps back to hidari jodan gamae.

Shidachi: Migi seigan gamae.

#35

Uchidachi: Right foot steps forward, shomen uchi (straight cut).

Shidachi: Left foot shuffles diagonally forward, block straight cut.

#36

Uchidachi: Continue straight cut.

Shidachi: Right foot steps forward, flip sword to seigan position.

#39

Uchidachi: Right foot steps forward, shomen uchi (straight cut).

Shidachi: Left foot shuffles diagonally back, kasumi uke.

#40

Uchidachi: Continue shomen uchi.

Shidachi: Raise sword to migi jodan gamae.

#41

Uchidachi: Finish shomen uchi.

Shidachi: Shuffle forward, shomen uchi.

#42

Uchidachi: Right foot steps back to migi hasso gamae.

Shidachi: Shuffle back to migi seigan gamae.

#43 *Return to starting position*
Uchidachi: Migi hasso gamae.

Shidachi: Right foot step back to hidari seigan gamae.

試し斬り

Chapter Eleven
Tameshigiri

1994 Kabutowari test
Taken at Jones Intercable Studios

Tameshigiri - Test cutting

Learning and maintaining precise technique is important throughout all levels of Shinkendo training, and test cutting serves as an important tool in this process. As a student begins to feel confident in their form and execution of kata, test cutting will graphically display the effectiveness of the student's grip, cutting edge angle, ability to judge distance, body physics and ability to stop the sword. Other elements of a cut, such as the quality of sound generated and the resistance felt while cutting are also accurate methods of evaluating technique. Through the study of tameshigiri, it will become apparent quickly whether the necessary fundamental skills have been attained.

It has been said that training in swordsmanship without the incorporation of test cutting is comparable to practicing combative shooting methods without firing a gun. Both require the application of principles to truly master the weapon. In swordsmanship, like firearms, it is important to study under a licensed and qualified instructor. Under a skilled instructor, swordsmanship should be practiced based on the principles discovered from tameshigiri; but only after the other elements of basic *toho jusshinho* (ten sword methods) have been studied. Swords and guns are alike in that they are inherently dangerous, and if handled without proper training, they can be dangerous to the user as well as to training partners and spectators. While skills are being honed, the temptation to speed up movements such as drawing and sheathing the sword or the rapid cutting of multiple targets must be resisted. It is far better to practice at 80% of the maximum speed and power possible than to push oneself to 100% and risk an accident. Students who have not trained under an experienced instructor that is qualified to teach tameshigiri should *not* attempt test cutting. A good instructor understands not only swords and techniques, but also the intricacies of human beings, has an awareness of potential safety liabilities, and is able to pass these important elements on to future generations of *kenshi* (swords practitioner).

With proper practice, anyone can cut soft material, such as dampened straw, using the razor sharp edge of a Japanese style sword. But training in tameshigiri is only one element of sword study, and as such the practitioner should not become infatuated with simply cutting targets. Shinkendoka should keep in mind the original purpose for tameshigiri training while practicing target cutting.

The goal of tameshigiri is to determine if one's overall toho jusshinho is correct, based on the lessons introduced by the serious study of tameshigiri.

Injuries should never be a part of normal practice. It is not acceptable to only cause injury to oneself one time out of every hundred repetitions of a given technique. Furthermore, swords practitioners should refrain from reckless displays of technique, such as cutting fruit or other objects held on people's bodies; a practice reminiscent of circus acts and sideshows. These displays are inherently dangerous and show a total lack of respect for the art of swordsmanship and the

history it represents. The study of the sword is an art form, and should be practiced with the utmost dignity and respect.

Kihon Shikon
The Four Fundamentals

1) Taisabaki- body movement practice; bio-mechanics of developing smooth,
fast and powerful body movements and understanding the principles of leverage.

2) Ashisabaki- leg, or foot movement practice; adjusting distance, weight
shifting, generating speed and balance through the study of footwork.

3) Kensabaki- sword movement practice; efficient manipulation of the
sword's weight, balance, cutting, blocking, parrying and thrusting capabilities.

4) Toho-jusshinho-The Ten basic methods of the sword:

1. Tenouchi-	Proper grip
2. Maai-	Distance to the target
3. Awase-	Various methods of timing the step/body movement in relation to the sword swing
4. Hohaba-	Stance and balance
5. Tachisuji (Tosen)-	Quality of the swing, or cutting line
6. Hasuji-	Adjustments to the angle of the blade's edge
7. Kakudo-	Angle of swing
8. Jushin no ido-	Shifting and rotating the body's center
9. Tome-	Ability to stop the sword upon completion of a swing
10. Nagashi, Kaeshi and Makuri	Methods of transitioning between cuts

Tenouchi- The proper basic grip for the left hand is to hold the hilt at the
bottom end (but not hanging over), then add the right hand above it with about a
two or three finger distance between them. The correct grip should be angled
naturally, with the forefinger of the right hand slightly touching the tsuba, but
excluding contact between the tsuba and thumb. Rotate both wrists inwards
(shibori) and position the goukoku (web between the thumb and first finger)in line
with the mune (back of the blade). If the nakago (tang) of your sword is too short,
the left hand should move closer to the right hand, to avoid breaking the wooden
tsuka (hilt) when cutting. This type of grip reduces the ability to stop a swing
cleanly, so care should be taken if this grip is used. The proper method of gripping the sword is crucial to providing the leverage and angles necessary to cut

accurately and stop the sword after cutting. Tenouchi and hasuji are closely related. Neglecting to maintain proper grip can cause varying degrees of *hirauchi*, or hitting the target with the side of the blade.

Maai- In this context, there are two types of maai to be concerned with: the distance from one's body to the target, and the distance of the *monouchi* (cutting area of the sword) to the target. The distance of the body from the target is slightly different from person to person, and can only be understood through practice. The monouchi generally is the last one-third of the blade, excluding the tip area. Of course, any part of the edge can be used to cut, but the monouchi has proven to be the part of the blade that provides the most cutting power, while minimizing the risk of the sword breaking or bending.

Awase- The difference in timing between the sword swing and that of the advancing/retreating foot should be adjusted to correspond to the type of cut performed. A cut is comprised of varying ratios of power and speed. A cut followed immediately by a step (as seen often in kendo) provides a great deal of speed, but not as much power. To complete a step and cut at the same time is most common, and generally provides an equal degree of power and speed. The third method, stepping and immediately afterward completing the cut, leave the body open for attack, but provides a great deal of power, at a slightly reduced speed. Additionally, when cutting kesagiri, one should be careful not to cut toward the forward leg. For example, when performing a right kesagiri, the right foot should be forward. In time of war many soldiers injured themselves by cutting their own foot or leg as a result of having the opposite leg forward.

Hohaba-One's weight should be balanced forward at all times to allow for rapid movement changes in any direction and to assist with cutting leverage. To achieve a stance that has sixty percent of the body weight forward, the feet should be about one and a half feet apart, much like that of a normal walking stride, with the weight over the front knee. The preferred cutting stance has seventy percent of the body weight forward. In this case, the feet should be two and a half to three feet apart, similar to a stride made when walking briskly, again with the weight over the front knee. This position should feel like a natural stride when done correctly.

Tachisuji, or Tosen- Strive for *enkei tosen* (circular sword line). Extend your arms, throw the tip outward and use the weight of the sword combined with its centrifugal force to swing in a straight, unwavering line. The sword's hilt and tip must travel through the same line, or the target may be knocked over and/or the blade bent. Eventually, the practitioner will learn to use the natural power of the body to swing the sword. Those that lack polished tachisuji will appear off balance.

Hasuji- Adjustment of the cutting edge of the sword. Adjust the ha (sharpened edge) and mune to line up perfectly with the swing. Approach the target and make a linear attack with the sword. Practicing tameshigiri will quickly help one determine the accuracy of one's hasuji, and like an inaccurate tachisuji, can also produce adverse results should hasuji be lacking even slightly. Incidentally, there are some TV and film actors that have glamorized a reverse-grip on the sword while filming. It should be understood that this method greatly reduces power and control, as well as the ability to accurately adjust hasuji. Please do not emulate these kind of acrobatics, as they are quite dangerous and of no use to authentic swordsmanship.

Kakudo- The most natural cut is kesagiri, a diagonal cut from high to low. The best angle with which to cut a target using kesagiri is thirty-five degrees from the vertical center line. Of course, a soft target with negligible grain may be cut at forty-five or ninety degree angles as well. In the case of bamboo, thirty-five degree angles are the most effective for both kesagiri and kiriage (rising cut). Cutting hard bamboo at less than thirty-five degrees can cause the sword to deflect off the target, or, may redirect the sword to follow the grain down the center of the bamboo, causing the bamboo to split or tear. Swinging at the bamboo at angles exceeding forty-five degrees usually results in striking the bamboo, rather than cutting it, and will knock the bamboo over, sometimes chipping the sword blade as well.

Jushin-no ido- Target cutting should be practiced using the movement of the whole body in conjunction with the sword, rather than simply swinging the arms. Shinkendo cutting incorporates shifting the body's balance and weight to provide additional speed and power, as well as the slicing motion (pushing or pulling) necessary to cut, rather than chop, a target. When moving forward, backward, to the right or left, the body's centerline should pivot as though on a vertical axis, and not be allowed to shift excessively.

Tome- After cutting, the tip of the sword should never drop below knee level. The inability to stop a sword swing will result in either striking the ground (causing sword and/or floor damage) or one's training partner (causing an injury). Thus, proper tachiuchi can not be performed without tome.

Nagashi, kaeshi and makuri- After perfecting tome, the techniques of nagashi (flowing naturally between cuts), kaeshi (cut and return on the same swing line) and makuri (cut and continue around to starting kamae) can be explored. These techniques are more difficult to perform correctly, as they introduce additional factors to adjust for, when checking elements such as clean hasuji and tachisuji. For a practitioner that has not developed strong tome, practicing these kind of continuous techniques can be extremely dangerous. Again, having proper tenouchi is critical to prevent the sword from slipping out of the practitioner's hands, causing a general loss of control of the sword or a loss of the practitioner's balance (an extreme hazard to bystanders).

Additional considerations for advancing cutting ability.
1. **Ki** — Exert one's energy and intention fully.
2. **Kokoro-gamae** Exhibit determined, confident and powerful, yet calm spirit.
3. **Sokudo** — Appropriate, but not excessive speed.
4. **Chikara** — Appropriate, but not excessive power.

Practitioners must strive to combine their understanding of these four elements with that of the closely related kihon shikon explained previously.

When the proper combination of all these elements has been achieved, one can truly perform sharp, safe and dignified sword techniques.

Practice can and should be done with a bokuto and iaito first, handling them as if they were a live blade. Once tameshigiri has been experienced, the knowledge and feeling gained from it should be applied to practice at all times, regardless of whether a bokuto, iaito or shinken is used.

•Test cutting Safety•

To safely learn test cutting requires an experienced instructor, a good blade (including adequate mountings, saya and hilt), skill with a sword and proper sword etiquette. This will minimize the chances of injury to self, or others.

Precautions to consider prior to test cutting

1. Pick a suitable location.
2. Carefully check the condition of the sword each session (retaining pin[s], edge, mouth and edge-side of the saya, etc.).
3. Assess the current condition of mind and body. It is not advisable to eat heavy food several hours before test cutting. A full stomach may make it more difficult to concentrate. Also, if one is under stress or lacking rest, one should postpone tameshigiri until the condition is rectified.

Position in front of target

1. Remain focused and calm.
2. Check surroundings for potential safety liabilities.
3. Perform several practice swings at the area of the target the cut is intended for, to check distance, grip, stepping method and stopping ability.

Cutting

1. Be full of spirit but relaxed - avoid becoming overzealous or anxious.

Upon completing a cut

1. Keep Zanshin and display dignity. Don't get overly enthusiastic about successful cuts, or visibly upset over unsuccessful cuts. Foster "heijyoshin" or even temperament.
2. Clean and care for the sword immediately after cutting sessions in an area safe from passersby.
3. At the first opportunity, reclean and double-check the condition of the sword.

Shinkendo Testcutting theories

The grip when cutting left kesagiri is more natural than that of right kesagiri, because of hand placement on the tsuka (handle). This allows for a tighter grip on left kesagiri, and the ability to adjust hasuji easily. However, right kesagiri is more powerful than left kesagiri. Additionally, stepping forward to cut (from either side) is more powerful than stepping back. Taking these facts into consideration, Shinkendo's basic testcutting techniques were structured with left kesagiri, stepping back first to insure safe practice. The new testcutting practitioner should not rely on power, but rather focus on correct posture and technique. In order to use targets economically and improve accuracy, students should perform at least four cuts per target, approximately ten centimeters apart (on tatami omote). Kesa cuts should be done accurately and consistently; avoid combining right and left side cuts diagonal cuts, as this takes up a significantly larger area of the target. Safety is of paramount importance, so instructors must carefully monitor the emotional condition of students and closely supervise them at all times.

Material

1. **Wara** - rice straw.
2. **Tatami Omote** - Igusa grass; the top layer of tatami floor boards.
3. **Medake** - narrow, soft green bamboo.
4. **Madake** - Japanese bamboo, with thinner walls than that found in moso dake.
5. **Moso dake** - Chinese bamboo. Usually a deep green in color and very dense.

Shinkendo Shizan Kihon Ichi

Ipponme - Facing the target, stand with your feet together and adjust the sword in relation to the target at chudan level. After establishing proper distance, take jodan-gamae and step back with the right foot, performing left kesagiri.

Nihonme- From feet together, sword at chudan level. Take jodan-gamae and step back with the left foot, cutting right kesagiri.

Sanbonme- Alternate stepping back, performing left kesagiri and right kesagiri.

Yonhonme- Take one step back- bring feet together, sword at chudan level. Take jodan-gamae, step forward with the left foot and perform left kesagiri.

Gohonme- From feet together, sword at chudan level. Take jodan-gamae, step forward with the right foot and perform right kesagiri.

Ropponme- Alternate stepping forward, performing left and right kesagiri.

Nanahonme- From feet together, step back with the left foot to assume a right chudan-gamae. Take right jodan-gamae (right foot forward) and step forward with left foot, cutting left kesagiri.

Happonme- Switch to right hasso-gamae (left foot forward). Take left jodan-gamae, step forward with the right foot and perform right kesagiri.

All of the above sets are performed with four cuts per target each placed approximately ten centimeters apart.

-Chiburi, noto, and clean sword.

Glossary

Ashi sabaki - foot work.

Bakufu - "tent government". A feudal military style of government.

Batto do - the art of drawing and and test cutting. Also called Battojutsu.

Battoho - combative drawing methods.

Bokuto - an older term for bokken, or "wooden sword".

Budo - military way/ techniques. Terms used to refer to Japanese martial arts. Also called "bujutsu".

Bushido - an Edo era term referring to the Bushido code of honor, behavior and general conduct.

Chiburi - "blood flicking" a finishing movement before resheathing.

Chudan gamae -a mid level posture with the sword tip pointing at the opponent's throat.

Chikara - power.

Dai-jodan gamae -similar to Jodan gamae, but with the tip held up vertically.

Dai no Budo - "large martial art". The effects of Budo on a larger scale.

Daimyo - a feudal era ruler of a fief or prefect.

Daisho - a matching pair of swords; wakizashi and katana.

Dan/kyu - The modern "black belt" ranking system used in many styles of Budo.

Dento - tradition.

Do-gi - uniform (top and bottom).

Dojo - "place to train in the way"; training hall or school.

Dotangiri - formal test cutting that incorporates a wider stance and powerful center cut.

Enkei tosen - circular sword-swing line.

Fuzoku - manner, custom.

Gedan gamae -low level posture with the sword tip about knee high.

Gyaku - opposite.

Gunto - military sword produced during the second World War.

Habaki - metal collar that fits on the sword blade and locks the sword in the scabbard.

Hakama - traditional split pants used in some traditional Japanese arts.

Hangetsu - "half moon". a Goho Battoho variation that includes a side cut.

Hasuji - "edge angle". The angle of a blade's cutting edge during a cut.

Heiho - fighting strategy.

Heijyoshin - even temperament.

Hidari - left.

Hirauchi - striking a target with the edge angled to either side, as opposed to inline with that of the swing. Often results in knocking the target over or bending the blade.

Hohaba - stance and balance.

173

Honbu - also written "Hombu". Home dojo or headquarters.

Hyoshi - rhythm.

Iaido - the art of drawing, usually from seiza.

Iaito - an unsharpened replica katana-style practice sword.

Ichimonji - "first letter". Two directional suburi exercise.

Jiha - ritual suicide.

Jinchuro - the principle of using the power of the bodies center.

Jinsei - life.

Jodan gamae - high level posture in which the sword is raised above the head.

Jokyu - advanced.

Kabutowari - "helmet splitting". A traditional testcutting reserved for sword testers to determine the effectiveness of a given sword and/or helmet.

Kaeshi - cut and reverse-cut back up the same line.

Kaeshi uchi - similar to maki uchi, except the blade passes over the opposite side of the body.

Kagamiishi - "mirror-stone"; A two part kata (usen and sasen) focusing on control of movement.

Kaishaku - decapitation performed during ritual suicide.

Kaji - smith.

Kakudo - angle.

Kamae - a ready posture.

Kasumi - "mist" or "haze". A high position block used against overhead strikes.

Kata - a prearranged form.

Katana - A style of Japanese sword worn cutting edge up.

Katana kaji - swordsmith.

Katanakake - stand for holding swords.

Katsujinken - "sword that preserves life". One of two paths a swordsman can follow. Promoting dignity and love, cutting away at the greatest enemy; ones own ego. To cut away at the impurities. See also "Satsujinken".

Kendo - a competitive contact sport derived from japanese swordsmanship.

Kenjutsu - the use of an already drawn sword; an older term for sword fighting techniques.

Ken sabaki - sword movement.

Kesa giri - refers to the kesa robe worn by priests. A diagonal cut, usually 35 to 40 degrees, downward and to one side.

Kiai - a focused projection of energy and intention, usually vocalized.

Kihon - fundamental or basic.

Kiri age - "rising cut". Usually 35 to 40 degrees up, upward and to one side.

Kiri kaeshi - "returning cut". A defense that includes a kasumi block and return cut.

Koiguchi - mouth of the saya.

Koiguchi o-kiru - breaking the seal of a sword and its saya.

Kuyo Junikun -twelve precepts of the nine planets stratagem". The fundamental philosophical formula used in Shinkendo.

Ma-ai - distance or combative distance.

Maki osae - "wrap-control". A counter to a strike in which Shidachi moves around the blade.

Maki otoshi - "wrap-drop". A difficult counter that includes a block and counter attack in the same movement.

Maki uchi - a parry to an overhead strike, using a shuffling step. See also " kaeshi uchi".

Makuri - a cut that smoothly transitions into another cut without retracing the line of attack.

Mangetsu - "full moon". A variation of Goho Battoho that includes a rising cut.

Mekugi - small wooden peg that secures the sword blade to the hilt. Retaining peg.

Menuki - a charm, often an animal, placed under the wrap of a sword hilt.

Mesen - eye placement when facing an opponent.

Migi - right.

Mikiri - using exact manipulation of distance as a tactic in tachiuchi.

Monouchi - the last third of the blade used for cutting (not including the kissaki).

Mune - the back of a sword blade.

Nagashi - to flow, transition fluidly.

Nakago - tang of a sword.

Noto - to resheath the sword.

Nukitsuke - one handed draw and side cut (Goho battoho, Ipponme).

Nukiuchi - one handed left diagonal drawing and cut (Goho battoho, Yohonme).

Omote - to the front.

Oyowaza - applied techniques.

Reiho - etiquette, manner.

Riai - the application of a technique or art. Fundamental theory.

Ryusui - "running water". A basic tachiuchi form comprised of three sets.

Sageo - the cord that fastens the sword to the user.

Samurai - "to serve/ attend". The term used to denote the warrior class in feudal Japan.

Sasen - counter-clockwise. See also "Usen".

Satsujinken - "the sword that takes life". One of two paths a swordsman can follow. This path serves no higher purpose than to kill. See also "katsujinken".

Saya - sword scabbard.

Sayu - from left to right, or right to left.

Seido - system, method.

Seigan gamae -a variation of chudan gamae in which the sword is held diagonally.

Seiza - the proper kneeling position.

Sensei -	teacher or instructor.
Senpai -	a senior student in a dojo, school, company or other professions.
Shaku -	1 shaku = 10 sun = 100 bu = 30.3 cm = 11.93" (0.995')
Shidachi -	term used in swordsmanship to denote the person who performs a technique. (Usually the person who prevails). See also "uchidachi".
Shiho -	"four direction". Moving in four directions to improve balance and movement.
Shikko -	method of walking on the knees.
Shibori -	the wringing action of the hands on the tsuka that provides a strong, stable grip.
Shihan -	senior master level instructor.
Shinchokugiri -	vertical straight cut.
Shitoka -	a professional sword tester. This term should not be confused with swordsmen that practice cutting targets.
Sho no Budo -	"small martial art". The effects of Budo on a smaller scale.
Shogun -	"military commander".
Shomen -	front, forward. also "Mae".
Shugyo -	severe or austere training.
Soke -	the inheritor and/ or headmaster of some styles or ryu-ha.
Sokudo -	speed.
Sonkyo -	a squatting position.
Suburi -	methods of swinging the sword.
Suburito -	a large, heavy wooden bokuto used for developing power and proper movement.
Suki -	an opening in an opponents' defense.
Tachi -	an earlier version of Japanese sword that is worn edge down.
Tachiaigoshi -	1) usually a form of crouching on one knee in which one leg is slightly forward of the other. 2) any ready position for drawing a sword.
Tachikaze -	the "whooshing" sound a sword makes when swung.
Tachisuji -	the angle/ path the sword blade follows during a cut. Also refers to aspects of the swing technique. See also "Tosen".
Tachiuchi -	"sword-strike". The term used in Shinkendo for two person sparring.
Tai sabaki -	body movement.
Taito -	to wear the sword.
Tameshigiri -	test cutting; usually on human bodies, bamboo or tatami.
Tanren gata -	prearranged solo forms.
Tanryoku -	the energy used and projected while performing physical training.
Tanto -	a style of long dagger sometimes worn by Samurai.
Tatami omote -	the top layer of tatami floorboards rolled and used for tameshigiri.
Tenouchi -	the proper method of gripping a sword hilt.

Toho jusshinho -the ten basic methods of using the sword.

Toko - swordsmith that does not have disciples.

Tome - stopping the sword at the end of a swing.

Tosen - the angle / path the sword blade follows during a cut. See also "tachisuji".

Tosho - swordsmith that has disciples.

Tsuba - sword guard.

Tsubamegaeshi -"sparrow cut" A cut that reverses up the same path (eg: kesagiri/kiriage).

Tsugi ashi - sliding step.

Tsuka - a sword hilt.

Tsuka ito - the silk or leather cord that is used to wrap a sword hilt.

Tsuki - thrust.

Tsurugi - double edged straight sword.

Uchidachi - term used in swordsmanship to denote the person who receives a technique (usually the person who is defeated). See also "Shidachi"

Uchite - the attacker in a tachiuchi. See also "Ukete".

Ukete - the defender in a tachiuchi (does not parry or reverse).

Ura - to the rear.

Usen - clockwise. See also "Sasen".

Uchi-deshi - "live in student". An older system of apprenticeship.

Uchikomi - strike.

Waki - side.

Waki gamae - a position where the sword is held slightly behind and to one side of the body.

Wakizashi - short "companion" sword, usually worn with the katana.

Waza - technique.

Yoko giri - side cut.

Yoroi - a common word for armor.

Zanshin - "lingering awareness". The feeling of alertness found in combative situations. Most martial arts encourage this feeling while training.

Zarei - formal bow from seiza.

Published by:
International Shinkendo Federation
P.O. Box 2134
San Gabriel, California
91778 USA
Tel (626) 307-4347
www.Shinkendo.com
shinkendo@aol.com